ISBN 979-8-9879290-4-9
© Copyright Shaun Howe, 2024

Scriptural references pulled from:
Barrows, Cliff. *New King James Version Bible*. Thomas Nelson Produced by Christian Duplications International, 1983.

Written by Shaun Howe

Published by
Debarim Publishing, LLC
807 W Broadway
Spiro, OK 74959
www.debarimpublishing.com

I would like to thank my dear friend Byron W. Voorheis III and his wife Michelle A. Voorheis for both encouraging and enabling me to complete this book. It couldn't have been done without them.

ERROR OF THE LAWLESS

CONTENTS

How To Use This Book

I am coming from the premise that *all scripture is given by inspiration of God and is profitable for doctrine, for reproof, for correction, for instruction in righteousness.*[1] However, several verses we've all heard preached from the pulpit are presented with a very different, even contradictory, interpretation. This book is meant to be a fresh look at each section systematically, placing them back into the language, history, and context in which they were penned. I hope you will find this perspective enlightening and finally make the New Testament clear and no longer in conflict with itself and the rest of the Bible. I suspect you will also discover these sections' rich and valuable when we stop trying to twist them to fit our molds!

This book is structured not so much as a book to be read from front to back but as a reference text to help you look up a particular passage and find a perspective you likely won't hear in a typical Christian church. I've tried to compile and address every New Testament text I've ever heard used to promote a Christian Antinomian doctrine which is a Greek word meaning "against/instead of law." It teaches that one is no longer obligated to the standards of God's Law because one has been "set free" by grace. You may have heard a section used for this purpose that I have not. I apologize if this does not have *all* the answers.

---

[1] 2 Timothy 3:16

1

Keep in Mind
- These sections are arranged by order of book.
- Some sections listed in the table of contents do not have their entries; instead, they will refer you to an entry for a similar passage. I include these anyway so that a person looking to answer a specific question can find that answer elsewhere.
- The standard translation, unless stated otherwise, is NKJV.
- Quoted scripture will show up in italic font with a footnote at the bottom of the page for including book, chapter, and verse.
- Additional scriptural reference will be noted as (see [scripture]) and will appear in bold font.
- Not every explanation follows the same structure. The structure of an explanation will change based on whatever seems most fitting to explain it efficiently.

Matthew

Matthew 5:17 "Came to Fulfill"

[17] *"Do not think that I came to destroy the Law or the Prophets. I did not come to destroy but to fulfill.*

Assertion:

Some have said that because Jesus "fulfilled" the Law, we do not need to keep it. They say, "He did it, so we don't have to."

Response:

First, based on the plain textual contrast between "fulfill" and "destroy," there is certainly one thing that "fulfill" cannot mean: destroy.

Second, the Greek word for "fulfill" (πληρόω - plēroō) means to fill up to the fullest extent and has no connotation of making something void or no longer effective.

Third, as usual, context is critical. The following verses explain further what he was speaking of. [17] *"Do not think that I came to destroy the Law or the Prophets. I did not come to destroy but to fulfill. [18] For assuredly, I say to you, till heaven and earth pass away, one jot or one tittle will by no means pass from the law till all is fulfilled. [19] Whoever therefore breaks one of the least of these commandments, and teaches men so, shall be called least in the kingdom of heaven; but whoever does and teaches them, he shall be called great in the kingdom of heaven.*

I think, based on the meaning of the word πληρόω - plēroō and the immediate context of the section, the point here is that Christ is filling the Law, i.e., he is expounding on it and making clear the heart, or the intent, behind the words of the Law, not negating them.

Christ's life and ministry fulfill the Law. He lived a life that exemplified the Law in many ways. From the daily mundane decisions to the great prophetic images, Christ was a living, breathing manifestation of the perfect Law of God. He showed us how to rightly love God[2] and love our neighbor[3]. His life was the prophetic image of God's redemptive plan, which was achieved by means of God's holy days. He was our Passover Lamb[4], our unleavened bread, our First Fruits offering[5], the administrator of the Spirit at the Feast of Pentecost[6], the soon-to-be coronated King at the Day of Trumpets[7], the ultimate atonement for his people as the High priest of the Day of Atonement[8] and the one who will eternally tabernacle with us in the great Feast of Tabernacles.[9]

In all these ways, Christ fulfills the Law, and in none of these ways does he render that same Law void or irrelevant.

Matthew 5:38-42 "But I Tell You"

[38]*You have heard that it was said, 'An eye for an eye and a tooth for a tooth.'*
[39]*But I tell you not to resist an evil person. But whoever slaps you on your right cheek, turn the other to him also.* [40]*If anyone wants to sue you and take away your tunic, let him have your cloak also.* [41]*And whoever compels you to go one*

---

[2] John 5:36-47
[3] Luke 10:25-37
[4] 1 Corinthians 5:6-8, 1 Peter 1:19
[5] 1 Corinthians 15:20-23
[6] John 16:5-11, Acts 2:1-4
[7] 1 Thessalonians 4:16
[8] Hebrews 9:1-14
[9] Revelation 20

mile, go with him two. ⁴²Give to him who asks you, and from him who wants to borrow from you, do not turn away.

Assertion:

Some have said that when he says, "you have heard...but I say..." He is replacing the former commandment with another.

Response:

Jesus here references **Exodus 21:25, Leviticus 24:20, Deuteronomy 19:21**.

Firstly, altering God's commandments would be a sin (see **Deuteronomy 4:2**) and would thus taint his status as the spotless lamb who can take away the sin of the world. Just that quickly, the entire plan of redemption is undermined.

Secondly, note that certain Pharisees (those who were against him) took everything he said and tried to turn it against him (see **Matthew 26:61**) yet never threw this comment back at him. This should imply to us that nobody in his day took this to mean that he was replacing any of God's commandments.

Contextually, earlier in the chapter, he mentions that *"he did not come to destroy the Law but to fulfill it"* and then begins to do exactly that - to fill it, elaborating on various things regarding the Law and elements of their culture, such as *"You have heard that it was said to those of old, 'You shall not commit adultery.' But I say to you that whoever looks at a woman to lust for her has already committed adultery with her in his heart..."*[10] and *"You have heard that it was said to those of old, 'You shall not murder, and whoever murders will be in danger of the judgment.' But I say to you that whoever is angry with his brother without a cause shall be in danger of the judgment."* Therefore, this section is no different. Jesus teaches that though the Law says that reciprocal justice ("eye for an eye") is just and fair, there is a greater and deeper response that can be made. One can turn the other cheek and show mercy, just as God has done for His people innumerable times

---

[10] Matthew 5:27-28, Matthew 5:21-22a

before, thus *"blessing those who curse you"*[11]. In short, he puts it this way: "you can do what is just and fair, or you can be above that, and take on the nature and character of your heavenly Father who repetitively shows *you* immeasurable mercy."

Matthew 12:1-8 "Not Lawful on The Sabbath"

[1]*At that time, Jesus went through the grain fields on the Sabbath. And His disciples were hungry and began to pluck heads of grain and to eat.* [2]*And when the Pharisees saw it, they said to Him, "Look, Your disciples are doing what is not lawful to do on the Sabbath!"* [3]*But He said to them, "Have you not read what David did when he was hungry, he and those who were with him:* [4]*how he entered the house of God and ate the show bread which was not lawful for him to eat, nor for those who were with him, but only for the priests?* [5] *Or have you not read in the Law that on the Sabbath, the priests in the temple profane the Sabbath and are blameless?* [6] *Yet I say to you that in this place there is One greater than the temple.* [7] *But if you had known what this means, 'I desire mercy and not sacrifice,'*[12] *you would not have condemned the guiltless.* [8] *For the Son of Man is Lord even of the Sabbath."*

(see also **Mark 2:23-28, Luke 6:1-11**)

Assertion:

Some have stated that Jesus is breaking the Sabbath and thus setting it aside. This interpretation is problematic in several ways. Let's see what this section is telling us.

Response:

Firstly, and most importantly, if Jesus were truly disregarding the Sabbath, then he would also be in blatant violation of the Law, thus sinning, and, like in other examples given in this book, would now be disqualified as the sinless one to atone for the sins of the world.

Looking deeper, the examples Jesus brings are those of David and the priesthood. Let's take a moment to explore each of these.

---

[11] Matthew 5:44

[12] *1 Samuel 15:22*

6

David's story can be found in **1 Samuel 21:1-6**. David is on the run from Saul and comes to the Tabernacle. He asks Ahimelech, the priest, if food is available for him and his men. Ahimelech responds that there is no common bread, but only the bread that was taken from before the presence of the Lord. He then asks if David and his men have abstained from women; this is effectively asking if he and his men are "clean" and thus able to eat this sanctified bread.

There are two misconceptions to clear up here before we continue. David did not enter the Tabernacle, nor did they eat the bread in the Tabernacle. The bread has already been removed from the presence of the Lord and replaced with fresh bread. This was done weekly. (see **Leviticus 24:5-9**) Also, notice that David and his men are "ritually" clean and can consume holy food. *"[the bread is] in effect common, even though it was consecrated in the vessel this day."*[14] Typically, priests and their families consume this bread, but it is given to David in this instance. All this explanation demonstrates is that neither David nor the priests were flippantly ignoring God's commands but doing everything possible to obey them while maintaining his survival.

This is where we get to the interesting part. There is an underlying theme in God's Law that David clearly understood, and presumably, the priests understood as well. A thread running through the entirety of the Law is that life is sacred. Many of God's commands prove the fact that the sanctity of life must be maintained. Some have even suggested that the laws about one being in a state of clean or unclean are even derived from the idea of maintaining the sanctity of life.

---

[14] 1 Samuel 21:5b

*Looking at the qualifications for what makes one clean or unclean in scripture from a birds eye view, you will notice that a large majority deal with making contact with something dead, or a loss of bodily fluids. Ancient Israelites considered bodily fluids the essence of one's life (see Leviticus 17:11) and losing these fluids synonymous with losing a part of one's life. This is why one who was "lacking life" would not be allowed in the house of the God.

David understood the sanctity of God's dwelling, but he also understood the sanctity of his own and his men's lives. Therefore, he goes to the priests with a request to maintain his life. When the only available option is the consecrated bread, he accepts it, knowing that preserving these lives is of greater importance to God than the sanctity of this bread. Even with that, he does everything possible to offend as little as possible.

Regarding the priests working on the Sabbath, we encounter another interesting dynamic of applying God's Law. If you read through the Bible, particularly the books of the Law, you will find that the priests are called to serve always, even on the Sabbath, while the rest of God's people are resting. In some cases, there is more work to be done by the priests on the Sabbath![15] How is this permissible? How is this not a contradiction? I think here we are uncovering another precious truth of scripture.

First of all, the Hebrew word for Sabbath (Shabbat, שַׁ בָּ ת) means literally to cease, to cease from one's daily activities and make that day set apart (holy) from the others. It does not carry the connotation of rest in the sense of relaxation but in the sense of ceasing your life and its priorities to focus on God and His priorities for your life.

With this perspective in mind, it makes sense that the priests and Levites continue their work on the Sabbath day. The Levites are entrusted to serve the LORD. Their job is worship! Therefore, their work is not a violation of the Sabbath.

Now, apply this principle to the context of Matthew 12. Jesus' disciples are faithfully following Him and were hungry. I make the case that their obedience to the Master is an act of worship to the Lord, and their need to fill their stomachs is an application of preserving human life.

---

[15] Leviticus 24:8, Numbers 28:9-10

Thus, Jesus brings two examples from the scripture to point out the priority here and rebukes the Pharisees for not knowing how to discern such a thing.

Additionally, it is essential to understand what the Pharisees understood as "working on the Sabbath"[16]. The Pharisaical interpretation is extremely legalistic and rigid and thus lacks discernment with the nuance of scripture. I would make the case that picking grain as one walks does not qualify as "work," it certainly does not qualify as something that distracts from God's priorities in your life, given the circumstances in the text.

It's the same idea Jesus presents in **Matthew 23:23** when he says, *"...you pay tithe of mint and anise and cumin, and have neglected the weightier matters of the Law: justice and mercy and faith. These you ought to have done without leaving the others undone."* In like manner, Jesus does not say to disregard the Sabbath. Instead, he shows how to discern proper Sabbath observance.

The account in Mark includes the line: *And He said to them, "The Sabbath was made for man, and not man for the Sabbath.[17]* and then concludes, like Matthew, that *"Therefore the Son of Man is also Lord of the Sabbath."* The Sabbath was made for our sakes, for us to relate to and connect with God. The moment we take an approach like the Pharisees did and turned the Sabbath into a list of things forbidden to us, we've missed the point of the Sabbath completely.

Even traditional Judaism touches on this concept similarly: "Rabbi Jonathan ben Joseph said, 'For it is holy unto you; i.e., it [the Sabbath] is committed to your hands, not you to its hands.'"

---

[16] Look up "39 Melachot" for a complete list of rabbinically forbidden activities on Sabbath, to get a better understanding of what Jesus is addressing.

[17] Mark 2:27
Talmud, Yoma 85b

Matthew 15:1-20 "Transgress the Tradition of the Elders"

See **Mark 7:1-23**

Matthew 22:37-40 "Two Great Commandments"

37 Jesus said to him, "'You shall love the LORD your God with all your heart, with all your soul, and with all your mind.' 38 This is the first and great commandment. 39 And the second is like it: 'You shall love your neighbor as yourself.' 40 On these two commandments hang all the Law and the Prophets."

Assertion:

It has been said that Jesus removed all the details of the Law and replaced them with the command to love. Is that true?

Response:

This does not say these are the only commandments, important ones, or anything similar. This says that the point of the Law is love, and the rest of the Law describes how God defines that love toward Himself or each other. Without these instructions, we can do *"whatever is right in our own eyes."*[18]

---

[18] Deuteronomy 12:8, Judges 17:6

Mark

Mark 2:23-28 "Not Lawful on the Sabbath"

See **Matthew 12:1-8**

Mark 7:1-23 "Transgress the Tradition of the Elders"

Then the Pharisees and some of the scribes came together to Him, having come from Jerusalem. [2] Now when they saw some of His disciples eat bread with defiled, that is, with unwashed hands, they found fault. [3] For the Pharisees and all the Jews do not eat unless they wash their hands in a special way, holding the tradition of the elders. [4] When they come from the marketplace, they do not eat unless they wash. And there are many other things which they have received and hold, like the washing of cups, pitchers, copper vessels, and couches. [5] Then the Pharisees and scribes asked Him, "Why do Your disciples not walk according to the tradition of the elders but eat bread with unwashed hands?" [6] He answered and said to them, "Well did Isaiah prophesy of you hypocrites, as it is written: 'This people honors Me with their lips, But their heart is far from Me. [7] And in vain they worship Me, Teaching as doctrines the commandments of men.' [8] For laying aside the commandment of God, you hold the tradition of men —the washing of pitchers and cups, and many other such things you do." [9] He said to them, "All too well you reject the commandment of God, that you may keep your tradition. [10] For Moses said, 'Honor your father and your mother'; and, 'He who curses father or mother, let him be put to death.' [11] But you say, 'If a man says to his father or mother, "Whatever profit you might have received from me is Corban"—' (that is, a gift to God), [12] then you no longer let him do anything for his father or his mother, ¹³ making the word of God of no effect through your tradition which you have handed down. And many such things you do." ¹⁴ When He had called all the multitude to Himself, He said to them, "Hear Me, everyone, and understand: ¹⁵ There is nothing that enters a man from outside which can defile him; but the things which come out of him, those are the things that defile a man. ¹⁶ If anyone has ears to hear, let him hear!" ¹⁷ When He had entered a house away from the crowd, His disciples asked Him concerning the parable. ¹⁸ So He said to them, "Are you thus without understanding also? Do you not perceive that whatever enters a man from outside cannot defile him, ¹⁹ because it does not enter his heart but his stomach, and is eliminated, thus purifying all foods?" ²⁰ And He said, "What comes out of a man, that defiles a man. ²¹ For from within, out of the heart of men, proceed evil thoughts, adulteries, fornications, murders, ²² thefts, covetousness, wickedness, deceit, lewdness, an evil eye, blasphemy, pride, foolishness. ²³ All these evil things come from within and defile a man."

(see also **Matthew 15:1-20**)

Assertion:

People have said that because Jesus disregarded the Pharisees' rules, assuming the Pharisees' rules are derived from the Old Testament Law, Jesus disregards the Old Testament.

Response:

Judaism has what is called the Written Torah and the Oral Torah. The Written Torah is synonymous with the biblical Law/Law of Moses/Genesis - Deuteronomy. The Oral Torah is the compiled teachings and traditions of the rabbis. Today, the Oral Torah is also written, but in the first century, as the name implies, it was passed down exclusively orally.

Rabbinic Jews (a modern extension of ancient Pharisees) tend to uphold the Oral Torah higher than the written one, so when the two contradict, the rabbis' teaching will trump the Word of God. Jesus, however, holds the Word of God, the Written Torah, as the ultimate authority. This conflict is the context of this chapter.

Now, let's walk through the chapter and see how this plays out.

Verses 1-5: The Pharisees (today, Orthodox Jews) taught that clean food becomes unclean unless a very specific ritual washing followed by a blessing is performed first. The blessing goes as follows: *"Blessed are You, Lord, our God, King of the Universe, who has sanctified us with His commandments and commanded us concerning the washing of hands."*

You can search the scriptures for the rest of your life; you will never find such a commandment. Notice that in verse 5, the text records that the Pharisees attribute their statement's authority to the "tradition of the elders." They have made this precept and enforced it as if God Almighty had done so. They are putting words in God's mouth.

Verses 6-9: Jesus calls them hypocrites and makes a stand on the authority of the word of God above the word of man. He accuses them of *"laying aside the commandments of God so that they may keep their tradition."*

This shows us something that may surprise some, but it is a very important piece of information for understanding the ministry and teachings of Christ: Pharisees were professional sinners. In common church culture, people assume that the Pharisees were experts in the Law of God and followed it to a tee. In actuality, Pharisees are experts in the religion of their own making, which starts with the Torah but then supersedes it and alters it as is convenient for them. I strongly recommend that one who desires to understand the life and teachings of Jesus and the rest of the New Testament should take some time to become acquainted with Orthodox Judaism. Doing so will illuminate much of the New Testament scriptures.

Verses 10-13: Jesus brings another example of their rabbinic traditions, replacing and nullifying the Torah to better illustrate his point.

Verses 14-23: Jesus explains that true defilement does not come from a physical act. True defilement in the eyes of God comes from the heart of man. He points out that the Pharisees, by ignoring the word of God and replacing it with their customs, have entirely missed the point that the scriptures were trying to create in them. God seeks a humble heart of obedience and faithfulness. Thus, although they become more righteous in their own eyes by their strict adherence to their tradition, they have become defiled in their hearts in the eyes of God.

Jesus is not teaching about food or cleanliness; He is transcending that level. Jesus is explaining that what matters is the cleanliness of the heart and that, when applied correctly and followed faithfully, the Law of God will teach this and the basic physical things to us. *"If anyone has ears to hear, let him hear."*

There is a serious translation error in verse 19. The NKJV says, *"because it does not enter his heart but his stomach, and is eliminated, thus purifying all foods?"* Most translations render it similarly, probably for two reasons: 1) it fits the translator's theological presuppositions, and 2) to render it correctly is crude, and people don't like crude things in their bible.

Many translations will change the last phrase to say, "thus Jesus made all foods clean." The *"thus Jesus made"* part of that thought is only found in the translators' minds and not in the text itself. Therefore, we are left with something like "cleansing all foods" at the end of the verse. Additionally, the word the NKJV renders "eliminated" in Greek describes a place where human excrement is left, in the modern vernacular, the toilet. Therefore, when we look at the verse this way, it reads something like this: *"because it does not enter his heart but his stomach, and is left in the toilet, cleansing all foods."*

This changes everything! Suddenly, the verse does not have Jesus arbitrarily changing the Laws of the Father. Now, he explains that physical uncleanness is temporal and passing and that we must focus more on keeping the heart clean because that is the root issue! God desires that we repent of our selfish and pious ways and become humble and submissive to Him. In achieving this, God will have an individual who will rightly obey even the minutia of His Law (including eating according to His standards) and who will reflect His character, a true son or daughter!

Additional Notes:

The word "food" used in this section (or any other part of the New Testament) must be understood as the people in the story and the book's author would have understood it. "Food" in the mind of the first-century Jew was defined as things that God has already declared to be food[19]. This section is, after all, a story about a Jew addressing a group of Jews. Therefore, a pig, for example, is not food. So when verse 19 says, *"purifying all foods,"* it never refers to things the Father has already deemed not to be food.

To translate into modern thought, if you had someone visit your home and you told them to help themselves to the kitchen, you would not expect them to come back chewing on a cardboard box. There is a mutual and cultural understanding of what is and is not food.

---

[19] Leviticus 11, Deuteronomy 14

Luke

Luke 5:33-39 "New Wine into Old Wineskins"

³³ Then they said to Him, "Why do the disciples of John fast often and make prayers, and likewise those of the Pharisees, but Yours eat and drink?" ³⁴ And He said to them, "Can you make the friends of the bridegroom fast while the bridegroom is with them? ³⁵ "But the days will come when the bridegroom will be taken away from them; then they will fast in those days." ³⁶ Then He spoke a parable to them: "No one puts a piece from a new garment on an old one; otherwise the new makes a tear, and also the piece that was taken out of the new does not match the old. ³⁷ And no one puts new wine into old wineskins; or else the new wine will burst the wineskins and be spilled, and the wineskins will be ruined. ³⁸ But new wine must be put into new wineskins, and both are preserved. ³⁹ And no one, having drunk old wine, immediately desires new; for he says, 'The old is better.'"

(see also **Matthew 9:14-17, Mark 2:18-22**)

Assertion:

Many mainstream Christian teachers will say that the "old" and "new" cloths and wineskins mentioned here are the old and new covenants, and Jesus is teaching that they are incompatible. Let's put this theory to the test:

Response:

Firstly, The bible being separated as the "Old" and "New"

testaments originated by Marcion[20] in the 2nd century, who taught that the God of the Old Testament was evil and inferior to the God of the New. Before that, such an idea had not been proposed. Marcion used the now popular interpretation of this passage as part of his argument, saying that the new cloth and the new wine are the new covenant by the new God and that the new is incompatible with the old. Marcion was universally accepted as a heretical teacher in his time, and he is still today. Remember, a bad tree does not bear good fruit.

The Bible's covenants do not contradict but complement each other. Also, remember Jesus' final statement, *"The old is better,"* or in some other manuscripts, *"The old is good."* This does not fit Marcion's and the modern church's interpretation that the old is inferior.

So then, what does this passage mean? Indeed, this passage has seen many different interpretations. I propose this:

The Pharisees have just asked Jesus why their disciples fast, and John's (the Baptist) disciples fast, but Jesus' disciples do not fast. He explains that they have no purpose in practicing such a thing right now because the bridegroom (himself) is still with them. Fasting is done in scripture as an act of mourning, and they have nothing to mourn.

This dialog with the Pharisees is the context for Jesus' parable. Jesus explains, by his parable, that his disciples are blue-collar people who have not been extensively trained in theology like those of the Pharisees or of John. They are a "blank slate." I have to believe that Jesus did this very intentionally. He did not want to train people who were already filled with preconceptions and ideas about how this "ought to be." The other side of this is that his disciples are undisciplined and untried in more difficult matters, such as fasting.

Therefore, his disciples lack both the reason and the training to fast

---

[20] Marcion also had his own canon, consisting exclusively of only ten of Paul's epistles and a gospel of Marcion's own making.

the way that the Pharisees and John did. (Traditionally, they fast twice a week.) Jesus also states that *"the days will come when the bridegroom will be taken away from them; then they will fast in those days."* This is to say that when they have been further trained and when the circumstances have changed, they will also fast.

So then, what are we to make of the details of the parable itself? Cloth tends to shrink as it is worn and washed repeatedly. If one were to put a brand new piece of cloth on a garment that has already been shrunk by usage, when the new patch began to shrink, it would pull away from the old garment and rip open.

Likewise, wine was often stored in wineskin (animal bladders). New (unfermented) wine must be put into new wineskins because the wine will ferment and expand, and the wineskins must also be able to expand. An old wineskin has already expanded, and if put to the test of expanding again, it will certainly burst open.

These parables simply explain how one should not impose behaviors of mature faith on one who is immature. It merely is inappropriate and may cause the vessels to "burst." In this way, the old is better because maturity is always preferred but cannot be forced before its time.

Luke 6:1-11 "Not Lawful on the Sabbath"

See **Matthew 12:1-8**

John

John 1:17 "But Grace and Truth Through Jesus"

¹⁷*For the Law was given through Moses, but grace and truth came through Jesus Christ.*

Assertion:

Because this verse says that grace came through Jesus, and some also see grace as juxtaposed to law, they conclude that Jesus brought something diametrically opposed to law, thus voiding law.

Response:

Some translations include a "but" between the two statements, which does not appear in the Greek. However, that doesn't entirely answer the question. Some may still say, even without the "but," that this verse creates a tension between law and grace.

The Law was indeed given through Moses, yet, as we know, the source of the Law was God Himself. When Jesus came, he came to bestow "grace and truth." In other words, he came to pour out the Spirit of "grace" (see **Zechariah 12:1**) and "truth" (see **John 14:17, John 15:26**). The "spirit of grace and truth," I would say, is a reference to the Holy Spirit. Jesus says, *"But when the Helper comes, whom I shall send to you from the Father, the Spirit of truth who proceeds from the Father, He will testify of Me"* (see also **Luke 24:49, Acts 1:4-8, Acts 2:4**)

A few verses earlier in **John 1:12-13** say, *"But as many as received Him, to them He gave the right to become children of God, to those who believe in His name: who were born, not of blood, nor of the will of the flesh, nor the will of man, but of God."*

How does one become a child of God? Paul explains in **Romans 8:14,** *"For as many as are led by the Spirit of God, these are sons of God."* Ezekiel prophesies that God would send His Spirit to lead us to follow His Law (see **Ezekiel 36:26-27**). Evidence that the Spirit is in us is found in the fact that we, as children of God, would obey His Law (see **Romans 8:4-8**).

What came through Moses and what came through Jesus should not be seen as opposing but rather as complimenting each other. Because the people with Moses lacked faith (see **Hebrews 4:2**), they didn't fully receive the Spirit, although a select few did (see **Numbers 11:25-30**). Thus, the Law alone came through Moses, but both the Spirit and truth (the Law) came through Jesus. To be more straightforward, one might put it this way: "Moses gave us God's instructions, but Christ animated the instructions for us."

John 7:21-24 "Made a Man Well on the Sabbath"

[21] *Jesus answered and said to them, "I did one work, and you all marvel.* [22] *Moses therefore gave you circumcision (not that it is from Moses, but from the fathers, and you circumcise a man on the Sabbath.* [23] *If a man receives circumcision on the Sabbath, so that the Law of Moses should not be broken, are you angry with Me because I made a man completely well on the Sabbath?* [24] *Do not judge according to appearance, but judge with righteous judgment."*

Assertion:
Because Jesus performs miracles on the Sabbath, some have asserted that he is breaking the Sabbath and making a statement about its irrelevance in doing so. Is that correct?

---

[21] John 15:26

Response:

The gospels are rife with Jesus discerning the gray areas of the Law to get to the heart of it. This is just another example. Technically speaking, the Law never prohibited circumcising on the Sabbath. Jesus thus draws a parallel, saying that it is acceptable to do a good and lawful thing on the Sabbath. Healing a person any day of the week is not a sin. "Judge with righteous judgment" is key. How does God define judgment?

[9] "Thus says the LORD of hosts: 'Execute true justice, show mercy and compassion everyone to his brother. [10] Do not oppress the widow or the fatherless, the alien or the poor. Let none of you plan evil in his heart against his brother'" [22] True judgment is to show mercy and compassion.

John 8:1-11 "Woman Caught in Adultery"

[1] But Jesus went to the Mount of Olives. [2] Now early in the morning, He came again into the temple, and all the people came to Him; and He sat down and taught them. [3] Then the scribes and Pharisees brought to Him a woman caught in adultery. And when they had set her in the midst, [4] they said to Him, "Teacher, this woman was caught in adultery, in the very act. [5] Now Moses, in the Law, commanded us that such should be stoned. But what do You say?" [6] This they said, testing Him, that they might have something of which to accuse Him. But Jesus stooped down and wrote on the ground with His finger, as though He did not hear. [7] So when they continued asking Him, He raised Himself up and said to them, "He who is without sin among you, let him throw a stone at her first." [8] And again He stooped down and wrote on the ground. [9] Then those who heard it, being convicted by their conscience, went out one by one, beginning with the oldest even to the last. And Jesus was left alone, and the woman standing in the midst. [10] When Jesus had raised Himself up and saw no one but the woman, He said to her, "Woman, where are those accusers of yours? Has no one condemned you?" [11] She said, "No one, Lord." And Jesus said to her, "Neither do I condemn you; go and sin no more."

Assertion:

Because the text says that the Law says that this woman should be stoned, and Jesus does not enforce that, people have stated that Jesus is

---

[22] Zechariah 7:9-10

consciously not applying the Law but choosing to ignore it.

Response:
First and foremost, it is essential to know that some manuscripts do not include 7:53–8:11; others add the passage here or after 7:36 or after 21:25 or after Luke 21:38, with variations in the text, but we will continue with this text assuming it is authentic.

Before we even get into the details, notice the motives of the Pharisees in verse 6: *"This they said, testing Him, that they might have something of which to accuse Him."* This episode happened not because of a desire for true justice but as a trap to ensnare Jesus.

By biblical Law, the woman did deserve to be stoned <u>if</u> and only if it could be legally proven that she was an adulteress *and* if the adulterer was present and proven guilty as well. God knew that the death penalty was a very serious ruling, so He put checks and precautions in place to save innocent people from being murdered by their vindictive neighbors.

The first and ominous problem with this circumstance is the lack of a man. By biblical Law, adultery requires both the man and the woman to be tried and, if proven to be true, executed (see **Deuteronomy 22:22**). What we see here is a woman but no man. Something is suspicious here. If Jesus were to condemn her without the man, he would not be adhering to biblical Law.

Additionally, the text says that she was caught in adultery, but it does not specify if the witnesses were present with them or how many there were. Biblical Law specifies that there be at least two or three witnesses and that they are present in the judgment (see **Deuteronomy 17:6-7, Deuteronomy 19:15**). That may or may not be an issue here, as the text does not give us that detail.

The curious part is what comes next; Jesus does not respond to them but begins writing on the ground. We're not told what he wrote, but whatever it was made the accusers feel "convicted by their consciences" and leave. I theorize that it was likely a member of the Pharisees themselves that enticed this woman undercover as a trap, and when they "caught her in the very act," it was because the whole thing was a setup. If this were to be the case, then the man who must be present and guilty of the same crime as this woman is among them, and they would be judged the same way they intend to judge this woman. Again, this is all speculation, but it could make a lot of sense.

Regardless of the validity of my own speculation, the text is clear that there was insufficient evidence, suspects, witnesses, or motives to make this case legal by biblical standards.

John 19:30 "It is finished!"

So when Jesus had received the sour wine, He said, "It is finished!" And bowing His head, He gave up His spirit.

Assertion:

Some have interpreted Jesus' last words here as referring to the fulfillment of the old covenant, which ended at his death. Let's examine.

Response:

Some have taken the phrase "It is finished" to be a reference to Jesus' death as the ultimate sacrifice (which it is) and thus conclude that all of the Old Testament sacrificial system, and by extension the Old Covenant as a whole, is now "fulfilled" by which they mean "made void" (see response on **Matthew 5:17**). Quite simply, this does not nullify any part of the old covenant, but it does say that what Jesus came to Earth to do and everything that encompasses it is now complete. Much like in **Matthew 5:17**, his ministry is not that of destroying what his Father had laid down prior in history but of expanding and enriching it.

Acts

Acts 10:9-29 "I Have Never Eaten Anything Common or Unclean"

⁹ The next day, as they went on their journey and drew near the city, Peter went up on the housetop to pray, about the sixth hour. ¹⁰ Then he became very hungry and wanted to eat; but while they made ready, he fell into a trance ¹¹ and saw heaven opened and an object like a great sheet bound at the four corners, descending to him and let down to the earth. ¹² In it were all kinds of four-footed animals of the earth, wild beasts, creeping things, and birds of the air. ¹³ And a voice came to him, "Rise, Peter; kill and eat." ¹⁴ But Peter said, "Not so, Lord! For I have never eaten anything common or unclean." ¹⁵ And a voice spoke to him again the second time, "What God has cleansed you must not call common." ¹⁶ This was done three times. And the object was taken up into heaven again. ¹⁷ Now while Peter wondered within himself what this vision which he had seen meant, behold, the men who had been sent from Cornelius had made inquiry for Simon's house, and stood before the gate. ¹⁸ And they called and asked whether Simon, whose surname was Peter, was lodging there. ¹⁹ While Peter thought about the vision, the Spirit said to him, "Behold, three men are seeking you. ²⁰ Arise therefore, go down and go with them, doubting nothing; for I have sent them." ²¹ Then Peter went down to the men who had been sent to him from Cornelius, and said, "Yes, I am he whom you seek. For what reason have you come?" ²² And they said, "Cornelius the centurion, a just man, one who fears God and has a good reputation among all the nation of the Jews, was divinely instructed by a holy angel to summon you to his house, and to hear words from you." ²³ Then he invited them in and lodged them. On the next day Peter went away with them, *and some brethren from Joppa accompanied him. ^{24} And the following day they entered Caesarea. Now Cornelius was waiting for them, and had called together his relatives and close friends. ^{25} As Peter was coming in, Cornelius met him and fell down at his feet and worshiped him. ^{26} But Peter lifted him up, saying, "Stand up; I myself am also a man." ^{27} And as he talked with him, he went in and found many who had come together. ^{28} Then he said to them, "You know how unlawful it is for a Jewish man to keep company with or go to one of another nation. But God has shown me that I should not call any man common or unclean. ^{29} Therefore I came without objection as soon as I was sent for. I ask, then, for what reason have you sent for me?"*

Assertion:

Because Peter was told to eat something unclean, it is assumed that the Spirit instructed him to break God's Law. Is that really what this text is about, though?

Response:

So here we have a section where Peter receives a vision wherein he is instructed to kill and eat unclean animals by a heavenly voice. Certainly, God is telling Peter to grill up some pork chops, right? Let's take a close look at the text and see if that's really why God sent this vision to Peter.

Verses 1-8: (Not shown above) The chapter begins with a story about Cornelius, the God-fearing gentile, praying. An angel comes to him and tells him his prayer was heard and that he should go and look for Peter. It should be clear that the rest of the chapter is connected to this event.

Verses 9-13: Peter is on the roof praying and is hungry. It is, after all, about midday and normal time for a meal. Peter then receives a vision of (clean and unclean) animals descending from heaven on a sheet with the instruction to *"kill and eat,"* repeated three times.

Verse 14: This is often overlooked. Peter immediately responds that he has never eaten anything common or unclean. This event happened roughly ten years after Jesus ascended back to heaven. Did Peter miss the memo that everything is clean now, or perhaps Jesus forgot to tell everyone, so he had to send an angel back? Perhaps we should keep reading.

Verse 15: *"What God has cleansed you must not call common."* This is the point of this vision. Keep it in mind.

Verse 16: Repetition is a common method in scripture to emphasize something. Thus, the vision is repeated three times.

Verse 17a: Peter wondered what it meant, which tells us that it was not an obvious interpretation like we all seem to hear today.

Verses 17b-28a: "Coincidentally," while Peter considered this vision, three men sent from Cornelius, the gentile introduced at the beginning of the chapter, came to the gate, seeking him. When he speaks to them, he hears about Cornelius' vision and travels with these men to meet Cornelius the next day. In Jewish culture, Gentiles were viewed as unclean simply because they were Gentiles, and they partook in several things that the Law says are unclean. Because of this, it was not socially acceptable for a Jew to enter the house of a Gentile (amongst other things). This is why Peter says, *"You know how unlawful it is for a Jewish man to keep company with or go to one of another nation."* **(**This is also the same problem Paul rebuked Peter for in **Galatians 2:11-16**.)

But Peter continues, *"God has shown me that I should not call any man common or unclean."* Now Peter understands the vision! The mixture of clean and unclean animals that Peter sees are the people that Peter is sent to preach to, Jews and Gentiles alike! It was shown to him three times to represent the three men seeking him.

Peter's vision was written for our understanding as well. We should never discriminate who we preach to; the gospel is for all! When Peter finally understands the vision, you will notice he does not go out to the market to buy pork chops. He never mentions meat at all. The text never says anything about declaring unclean meats suddenly clean but rather declaring so-called unclean people as clean.

Verse 28: Who are we to re-interpret this vision to mean something completely different? To do so suggests that we can interpret Peter's vision better than Peter.

This is not the first time God has used the act of eating things that are not food as a metaphor to teach a greater point. God commands both Ezekiel and John in a vision to eat a scroll (see **Ezekiel 3:1-4, Revelation 10:8-10**). This does not make scrolls food now. It's a vision; it's meant to represent something more significant.

Acts 15:1-20 "Unless you are Circumcised you Cannot be Saved"

And certain men came down from Judea and taught the brethren, "Unless you are circumcised according to the custom of Moses, you cannot be saved." [2] Therefore, when Paul and Barnabas had no small dissension and dispute with them, they determined that Paul and Barnabas and certain others of them should go up to Jerusalem, to the apostles and elders, about this question. [3] So, being sent on their way by the church, they passed through Phoenicia and Samaria, describing the conversion of the Gentiles; and they caused great joy to all the brethren. [4] And when they had come to Jerusalem, they were received by the church and the apostles and the elders; and they reported all things that God had done with them. [5] But some of the sect of the Pharisees who believed rose up, saying, "It is necessary to circumcise them, and to command them to keep the Law of Moses." [6] Now the apostles and elders came together to consider this matter. [7] And when there had been much dispute, Peter rose up and said to them: "Men and brethren, you know that a good while ago God chose among us, that by my mouth the Gentiles should hear the word of the gospel and believe. [8] So God, who knows the heart, acknowledged them by giving them the Holy Spirit, just as He did to us, [9] and made no distinction between us and them, purifying their hearts by faith. [10] Now therefore, why do you test God by putting a yoke on the neck of the disciples which neither our fathers nor we were able to bear? [11] But we believe that through the grace of the Lord Jesus Christ we shall be saved in the same manner as they." [12] Then all the multitude kept silent and listened to Barnabas and Paul declaring how many miracles and wonders God had worked through them among the Gentiles. [13] And after they had become silent, James answered, saying, "Men and brethren, listen to me: [14] Simon has declared how God at the first visited the Gentiles to take out of them a people for His name. [15] And with this the words of the prophets agree, just as it is written:

¹⁶ 'After this I will return
And will rebuild the tabernacle of David, which has fallen down;
I will rebuild its ruins,
And I will set it up;
¹⁷ So that the rest of mankind may seek the Lord,
Even all the Gentiles who are called by My name,
Says the Lord who does all these things.'

¹⁸ "Known to God from eternity are all His works. ¹⁹ Therefore I judge that we should not trouble those from among the Gentiles who are turning to God, ²⁰ but that we write to them to abstain from things polluted by idols, from sexual immorality, from things strangled, and from blood. ²¹ For Moses has had throughout many generations those who preach him in every city, being read in the synagogues every Sabbath."

²² Then it pleased the apostles and elders, with the whole church, to send chosen men of their own company to Antioch with Paul and Barnabas, namely, Judas who was also named Barsabas, and Silas, leading men among the brethren.

²³ They wrote this letter by them:

The apostles, the elders, and the brethren,
To the brethren who are of the Gentiles in Antioch, Syria, and Cilicia:
Greetings.

²⁴ Since we have heard that some who went out from us have troubled you with words, unsettling your souls, saying, "You must be circumcised and keep the law"—to whom we gave no such commandment— ²⁵ it seemed good to us, being assembled with one accord, to send chosen men to you with our beloved Barnabas and Paul, ²⁶ men who have risked their lives for the name of our Lord Jesus Christ. ²⁷ We have therefore sent Judas and Silas, who will also report the same things by word of mouth. ²⁸ For it seemed good to the Holy Spirit, and to us, to lay upon you no greater burden than these necessary things: ²⁹ that you abstain from things offered to idols, from blood, from things strangled, and from sexual immorality. If you keep yourselves from these, you will do well. Farewell.

Assertion:

Because this section is so large, antinomians will draw a couple of points from it. For one, people will look at the first point: "You must be circumcised and keep the law to be saved," which is refuted in the chapter, thus concluding that the Law does not need to be observed at all! Secondly, people will point to the four rulings given by the apostles and then conclude that those are the only rulings we must observe, and we may, or even must, disregard all other biblical Law. Let's explore this fascinating section.

Response:

This is a pretty large section, so let's break it up and walk through it.

Verse 1: This is the background for all the events in this chapter. Men from Judea (later identified as believing Pharisees in verse 5) came and taught the believers that gentile converts must be circumcised and obey the Law to be saved. It is important to realize that circumcision in first-century Judea implied much more than just the surgical act. Circumcision in the first century was an identifying marker of a Jew practicing Judaism. To be circumcised meant culturally that you were Jewish, and to be Jewish meant that you followed a whole set of cultural guidelines laid down in large part by phariseeism. What these particular Pharisees are trying to teach is that a gentile must first become circumcised, that is, Jewish before Jesus can save them.

Verses 2-5: Paul and Barnabas disagree with these believing Pharisees and thus decide that they and some others should go to Jerusalem to meet with the church's elders to ensure that their opinions were not out of line. The Pharisees meet them there and say the same things.

Verses 6-17: The apostles gather to discuss this topic. Peter stands up and references the situation he experienced in Acts 10, how divine revelation taught him not to exclude Gentiles from coming to the body of faith. Paul and Barnabas describe their experiences teaching the Gentiles how God continuously brings miracles to testify of the message before the Gentiles. James references the words of the prophets (see **Amos 9:11-12** to validate the fact that God is calling and working with the Gentiles in the same way as he has done with the Jews.

Therefore, the *"yoke on the neck of the disciples which neither our fathers nor we were able to bear"* is likely a reference to Judaism. Judaism included a whole set of parameters that must be in place before a gentile can convert to Judaism, as well as many other things. Peter concludes that putting such a yoke on the neck of these newly converted Gentiles would overload them with things that even native Jews were not able to bear.

Verses 18-21: Here is the decision! James proposes that they write to the Gentiles and teach them to obey just these four things: *"abstain from things polluted by idols, from sexual immorality, from things strangled, and from blood."* These seem like a strange selection of things for the council to instruct the new Gentiles to do until we understand the culture in which these Gentiles lived. These Gentiles all grew up in a pagan culture. Pagan ritual was part of their everyday lives. These instructions are designed to remove the new converts from their pagan lifestyle. This is the first and highest priority to the apostles.

James then says that as the Gentiles attend synagogue every Sabbath, they will hear Moses read and learn the details over time. In the early days of the spread of the gospel, messianic believers, Jew and gentile alike, met in synagogues as just another Jewish sect. Over the first couple hundred years for a number of historical and cultural reasons, messianic believers separated from the synagogue, but during the time of Acts, and thus the writing of this passage, no such distinction has been made yet.

This is how we should always treat new believers: give them some basic starting principles and slowly teach them more as they continue their walk. Faith initiates salvation, and obedience follows after. The pharisaic approach says that obedience comes before salvation, contrary to the apostles' doctrine.

Verses 22-29: The apostles write a letter to the gentile believers in Antioch, Syria, and Cilicia and send it by the hands of select men explaining to them that they have heard and considered the matter of the believing Pharisees teaching that Gentiles should be circumcised and keep the Law to be saved. The apostles explain that they gave no such commandment and then explain that the Gentiles should focus first on the four basic things: abstain from things offered to idols, from blood, from things strangled, and from sexual immorality. If they start with these things, they *"will do well"* because they will have removed themselves from pagan culture and thought and will begin to be integrated into the culture and thought of the worship of the God of scripture.

Romans

Romans 2:12-15 "Gentiles Who Show the Work of the Law Written on Their Hearts"

[12] *For as many as have sinned without Law will also perish without Law, and as many as have sinned in the Law will be judged by the Law* [13] *for not the hearers of the Law are just in the sight of God, but the doers of the Law will be justified;* [14] *for when Gentiles, who do not have the Law, by nature do the things in the Law, these, although not having the Law, are a law to themselves,* [15] *who show the work of the Law written in their hearts, their conscience also bearing witness, and between themselves their thoughts accusing or else excusing them*

Assertion:

It has been said that because of this section, we do not need to obey the Law because the Gentiles in this passage never did, and God accepted them. This understanding is severely lacking in understanding the context of what Paul is teaching. Let's dig deeper.

Response:

Paul uses obedience to the Law as a gauge of one's heart. A person's actions will clearly show where their affections are. Like Jesus taught, *"A good tree cannot bear bad fruit, nor can a bad tree bear good fruit. "Every tree that does not bear good fruit is cut down and thrown into the fire. "Therefore by their fruits, you will know them.* "[23]

As Paul explains a few verses earlier: *"eternal life to those who by patient continuance in doing good seek for glory, honor, and immortality; but to those who are self-seeking and do not obey the truth, but obey unrighteousness--indignation and wrath, tribulation and anguish, on every soul of man who does evil"*[24] Thus, Paul rightly shows that one's justification does not come from the works that they do, but from the intentions of their heart and the intentions of one's heart can be seen by the works that they do. In short, works don't justify a person, but they do authenticate one's justification.

So, to apply this understanding of the context to the section in question, we can now see that obedience to the Law isn't at the heart of the matter. Obedience is symptomatic of a faithful and God-fearing heart. Thus, the Gentiles that do not have the Law show the work of the Law written on their hearts because they are those of faithfulness and a desire to serve the Lord in whatever capacity they can. This is all the Lord ever desired for His people. He says, *"And these words which I command you today shall be in your heart."*[25]

He wants us to internalize His will. He does not want to command us to do His wishes (like a slave master), but rather that we would "earnestly seek" to do what He wants (like a child toward it's parent or a bride toward her husband). For more on this topic, see the **Galatians 3:23-25** entry. If we have that heart that has internalized His will and have never seen a bible all our lives, we will still do our best to please Him in whatever way we can. Fortunately, He has made His word readily accessible to us so we *can* learn how to please Him the way He desires.

Romans 2:25-29 "Circumcision is that of the Heart"

[25] For circumcision is indeed profitable if you keep the Law; but if you are a breaker of the Law, your circumcision has become uncircumcision.[26] Therefore, if an uncircumcised man keeps the righteous requirements of the Law, will not his uncircumcision be counted as circumcision?[27] And will not

---

[23] Matthew 7:18-20

[24] Romans 2:7-9a

[25] Deuteronomy 6:6

*the physically uncircumcised, if he fulfills the Law, judge you who, even with
your written code and circumcision, are a transgressor of the Law? ²⁸ For he is not
a Jew who is one outwardly, nor is circumcision that which is outward in the
flesh; ²⁹ but he is a Jew who is one inwardly; and circumcision is that of the heart,
in the Spirit, not in the letter, whose praise is not from men but from God.*

Assertion:

Some have said that because circumcision is in the heart, then the
physical act of circumcision, and by extension, physically obeying any of
God's Law, is unnecessary. That is not what Paul is teaching. Let's
explore this passage:

Response:

In the larger context (see previous entry on **Romans 2:12-15**), Paul
discusses the dynamic between works and the heart's intentions. This
section is still on that subject. However, before progressing in this line of
thought, we must establish something first.

What does "circumcision" mean to a first-century Jew, such as Paul?
When we hear the word "circumcision," we think of a surgical procedure.
In the first-century Jewish world, circumcision was much more than a
procedure. It was a cultural identifier. To be circumcised, or to be "of the
circumcision," is to be a part of the Jewish culture and faith (see **Acts
10:45, 11:2, Romans 3:30, 4:9, 4:12, 15:8, Galatians 2:7-9, 2:12, Ephesians
2:11, Philippians 3:3, Colossians 4:11, Titus 1:10**). This is one of a rare few
passages in the New Testament that acknowledges the difference between
being called "circumcised" and undergoing the physical act of
circumcision (rare because it was well understood in culture, and didn't
need to be explained in most contexts). Paul will explain that the physical
act is not synonymous with being a "true Jew," even though that is how
it is culturally recognized.

Paul also speaks of a Jew in this passage in the idealistic sense. To Paul, a
Jew is a faithful adherent to the God of Israel. Paul uses the language of
"Jew" in this passage strictly in the religious sense, ignoring, for the time
being, the ethnic sense. In short, in this section, Jew means believer.

Now, we can continue. Paul says that being Jewish is profitable if you keep the Law, but if you are a breaker of the Law, you are not truly Jewish, not truly a believer, and your circumcision is invalid. On the other side, if one is physically uncircumcised but still keeps the Law, he is as though he were circumcised, even though he has not undergone the surgical procedure, because it is evident that his heart is "circumcised" (see **Deuteronomy 10:16 and 30:6, Jeremiah 4:4**) and thus is a true Jew/ believer. A true Jew/believer is not one who merely wears the symbols of a believer, such as circumcision. A true believer, a true Jew, is circumcised in the heart, in the Spirit (see **Deuteronomy 10:16 and 30:6, Jeremiah 4:4**).

Romans 3:19-22a "Under the Law, Righteousness of God Apart From the Law"

[19] *Now we know that whatever the Law says, it says to those who are under the Law, that every mouth may be stopped, and all the world may become guilty before God.* [20] *Therefore by the deeds of the Law no flesh will be justified in His sight, for by the Law is the knowledge of sin.* [21] *But now the righteousness of God apart from the Law is revealed, being witnessed by the Law and the Prophets,* [22] *even the righteousness of God, Through faith in Jesus Christ, to all and on all who believe.*

Assertion:
   If the Law shall justify no flesh, why bother with it?

Response:
   Being under the Law is shorthand for being under the curse of the Law, which came about through disobedience to the Law. Please see the explanation in **Galatians 5:18** for more on the phrase *"under the Law."*

"Whatever the Law says, it says to those who are under the Law," that is, those guilty of violating its terms. "Every mouth may be stopped, and all the world may become guilty before God." The Law will humble all of us because we all have transgressed the Law (i.e., committed "sin." see **1 John 3:4**), which the Law shows us clearly "for by the Law is the knowledge of sin." Therefore, no one can be justified by it because we all have failed at some point. Because of this, His righteousness was sent to us, separate from the works of the Law. By faith in His Messiah, we are

accounted righteous.

God knows we are imperfect in a fallen world and never expected lifelong behavioral perfection. Salvation is and was always by faith through both Testaments. We were never meant to be justified by any work. When we accept this faith, we are born again and become sanctified. We begin growing by His Spirit, moving into obedience (see **Ezekiel 36:26-27**).

The Father's ultimate aim is not to assemble a collection of robots who all do whatever He tells them. He is seeking a body of people who, with their minds and hearts, have chosen to be faithful to Him. The result may look similar, that is, a group of people who are obedient to God, but the motivation and the means to get to that end are entirely different.

Romans 3:28 "Justified by Faith, Apart from Law"

[28] *Therefore we conclude that a man is justified by faith apart from the deeds of the Law.*

Assertion:

Why keep the Law if it does not justify?

Response:

Indeed, the Law does not justify, but take it in context, specifically verse 31: *"Do we then make void the Law through faith? Certainly not! On the contrary, we establish the Law."* No level of obedience to the Law will save you. Paul knows this. Faith saves by grace alone. However, once faith is accepted, obedience is expected to follow. *"If you love me, keep my commandments."* [26]

The confusion comes when people get the cause and effect mixed up. Faith comes first, by means of grace, unto salvation. Sanctification by obedience follows after. When a person attempts to put sanctification or obedience first, excepting it to lead to salvation, they have betrayed the gospel message.

---

[26] John 14:15

Romans 4:15 "Law Brings about Wrath"

[15] because the Law brings about wrath; for where there is no Law there is no transgression.

Assertion:

If the Law brings about wrath, certainly it must be bad, right?

Response:

The Law brings about wrath when a person breaks it. Without rules, there is nothing to break; nothing to break means there is no reason for punishment. The Law brings about punishment only when it is broken. However, we have all broken the Law of God, and thus it incurs wrath on us all. Of course, God, as the perfect Father, set forth this Law to teach us because He loves us. His discipline is not bad (see **Proverbs 3:12, Hebrews 12:5-8**).

Romans 6:6-7 "Old Man has been Crucified"

[6] knowing this, that our old man was crucified with Him, that the body of sin might be done away with, that we should no longer be slaves of sin. [7] For he who has died has been freed from sin.

Assertion:

Some have claimed that the "old man" in this passage references the old covenant, which has, thus, died with Christ.

Response:

Consider a few verses earlier where Paul establishes what he is speaking of. *[1] What shall we say then? Shall we continue in sin that grace may abound? [2] Certainly not! How shall we who died to sin live any longer in it?*

[27] Our "old man" is the body of sin. Sin is transgression of the Law; [28] therefore, the old man who died is not the old covenant, but the old you, your sinful past.

---

[27] Romans 6:1-2
[28] 1 John 3:4

Romans 6:14 "Not Under Law"

[14] For sin shall not have dominion over you, for you are not under Law but under grace.

Assertion:

"You are not under Law" must mean that we aren't supposed to keep the Law, right?

Response:

Again, context is vital.

[12] Therefore do not let sin reign in your mortal body, that you should obey it in its lusts. [13] And do not present your members as instruments of unrighteousness to sin, but present yourselves to God as being alive from the dead, and your members as instruments of righteousness to God. [14] For sin shall not have dominion over you, for you are not under Law but under grace. [15] What then? Shall we sin because we are not under Law but under grace? Certainly not! [16] Do you not know that to whom you present yourselves slaves to obey, you are that one's slaves whom you obey, whether of sin leading to death, or of obedience leading to righteousness? [29]

Do not be a slave to sin (i.e., lawlessness, see **1 John 3:4**). Therefore, do not let sin be the master of your mortal body, and obeying it in its sinful temptations. You must be the master over it instead (see **Genesis 4:7**). Do not allow any part of your physical body to do anything unrighteous (sinful; unlawful), and do not let any part of your spiritual body (your congregation) do anything unrighteous (sinful; unlawful). Instead of sinning (acting lawlessly), present yourselves to God as people who have been reborn, spiritually resurrected with Christ, and thus freed from the bondage of sin, and that the parts of your bodies (physical and spiritual) may act as instruments of righteousness.

We do righteousness and put sin to death for God's sake (simply put, we stop sinning because He wants us to). God uses willing individuals to

---

[29] Romans 6:12-16

accomplish righteous acts on the earth. Therefore, do not let sin (lawlessness) have rule (authority) over you. Why should we not allow sin to rule over us? Because we are no longer under the servitude of the law of sin (see **John 8:34, Romans 6:18-22, Romans 7:23-25, Romans 8:2, 2 Peter 2:19**) but rather we are graciously given salvation from sin and its penalties. We are given reconciliation/reunion with God to have a perfect covenant relationship with Him.

What should we do now? Shall we sin (commit lawlessness) just because we are no longer under the justly-deserved punishment as stated in the Law? In other words, should we "do the crime" knowing that we won't have to "do the time"? Certainly not! Don't you know that if you present yourself to serve something, you will be a slave to that thing? If you present yourself as a servant to sin (lawlessness), your fate is death because death is the guaranteed result of intentional lawlessness (see **Romans 6:23, Deuteronomy 24:16, Ezekiel 3:18-19, Ezekiel 18:4, 20**). If you present yourself as a servant to obedience, your fate is Christ declaring you righteous (see **Romans 6:18**).

Romans 7 "Died to the Law"

(Due to the amount of verses taken from this chapter and the amount of context needed, we will just review the entire chapter piece by piece)

Assertion:
The chapter discusses being *"dead to the Law,"* so many conclude that that means we're not supposed to acknowledge the Law anymore.

Response:
Paul is getting deep into the theological jungle in this chapter. Let us take some time and explore the entire chapter, thought by thought.

Romans 7:1
[1] *Or do you not know, brethren (for I speak to those who know the Law), that the Law has dominion over a man as long as he lives?*

If you do not "know the Law," you will misunderstand what comes next.

To know the Law does not mean you've read it a few times. It means you've seriously studied it and lived it. It is like the difference between knowing someone you just recently met versus knowing your spouse.

Romans 7:2-3

² *For the woman who has a husband is bound by the Law to her husband as long as he lives. But if the husband dies, she is released from the law of her husband.* ³ *So then if, while her husband lives, she marries another man, she will be called an adulteress; but if her husband dies, she is free from that law, so that she is no adulteress, though she has married another man.*

Paul is setting the stage. He is now talking about the laws of marriage and divorce. This can be found in **Deuteronomy 24:1-4.** He also makes mention of this understanding in **1 Corinthians 7:39** when he says, *"A wife is bound by law as long as her husband lives; but if her husband dies, she is at liberty to be married to whom she wishes, only in the Lord."*

This, specifically, is the law that *"has dominion over a man as long as he lives"* from verse 1, the law about marriage. This section does not speak of the entirety of the biblical Law; it makes a theological point by using this particular set of laws about marriage as an illustration.

Romans 7:4

⁴ *Therefore, my brethren, you also have become dead to the law through the body of Christ, that you may be married to another—to Him who was raised from the dead, that we should bear fruit to God.*

Keeping with the context, the laws regarding marriage are being spoken of. Therefore, you have become dead to that law through Christ that you may be married to another. Am I trying to say that we no longer must observe laws about marriage? Not at all. Paul is speaking in metaphor. He isn't trying to change God's eternal Law but making a theological point about it.

Let's back up a little bit. Jeremiah 3 explains that God was in a marriage covenant with Israel and Judah. Jeremiah 3:8a says, "⁸ *Then I saw that for all the causes for which apostate Israel had committed adultery, I had put her away and given her a certificate of divorce."* God divorced Israel because of their harlotry. According to the Law in **Deuteronomy 24**, because Israel was acting as a harlot, simply put "cheating," Israel was not able to be remarried to her previous husband, who was God.

Then, just a couple of verses later, **Jeremiah 3:12** says, *"Return, apostate Israel."* By God's own Law, this isn't possible. God's Law states that: *"When a man takes a wife and marries her, and it happens that she finds no favor in his eyes because he has found some uncleanness in her, and he writes her a certificate of divorce, puts it in her hand, and sends her out of his house, when she has departed from his house, and goes and becomes another man's wife, if the latter husband detests her and writes her a certificate of divorce, puts it in her hand, and sends her out of his house, or if the latter husband dies who took her as his wife, then her former husband who divorced her must not take her back to be his wife after she has been defiled"* [30]

We, as a people, were once "married" to the LORD, but because of our spiritual adultery, the LORD had given us a certificate of divorce as we went off with our new spouse, idolatry. By God's Law, we are not permitted to return to him and are defiled. But God said He would take us back! How is this possible?

Paul explains that we have died with Christ and are now freed from the terms of our marriage that we were bound by. We are freed from *that* law so that we may legally be married to the Messiah! We, with our sins, have died with Christ to be reborn as a new creation, thus no longer under obligation to the law of marriage. Paul also states in **2 Corinthians 11:2**, *"For I am jealous for you with godly jealousy. For I have betrothed you to one husband, that I may present you as a chaste virgin to Christ."*

---

[30] Deuteronomy 24:1-4a

Romans 7:5-7

5 For when we were in the flesh, the sinful passions which were aroused by the Law were at work in our members to bear fruit to death. 6 But now we have been delivered from the Law, having died to what we were held by, so that we should serve in the newness of the Spirit and not in the oldness of the letter. 7 What shall we say then? Is the Law sin? Certainly not! On the contrary, I would not have known sin except through the Law. For I would not have known covetousness unless the Law had said, "You shall not covet."

The *"sinful passions aroused by the Law"* are simply our sinful nature to whatever selfish thing we desire. The Law came and gave guidelines about right and wrong, which conflicted with our own nature. Thus, the Law aroused our sinfulness. In this particular case, it is about the nature of spiritual adultery. The reason the Law arouses it is explained in verse seven: without rules, there is nothing to break, and with no rules to break, there is no sin. The Law's primary purpose is to define sin (see **1 John 3:4** and the entry on **Romans 4:15**). The Law does not create sin in us; it only identifies it.

Now, being dead to that law by dying to our "old man," our sinful nature, we can *"serve in the newness of the Spirit and not in the oldness of the letter."* Simply put, now we can serve the Lord afresh, with a heart that desires to do so, and not only because we are under covenant obligation to do so.

Romans 7:8-14

8 But sin, taking opportunity by the commandment, produced in me all manner of evil desire in me. For apart from the Law, sin was dead. 9 I was alive once without the Law, but when the commandment came, sin revived and I died. 10 And the commandment, which was to bring life, I found to bring death. 11 For sin, taking occasion by the commandment, deceived me, and by it killed me. 12 Therefore the Law is holy, and the commandment holy and just and good. 13 Has then what is good become death to me? Certainly not! But sin, that it might appear sin, was producing death in me through what is good, so that sin through the commandment might become exceedingly sinful. 14 For we know that the Law is spiritual, but I am carnal, sold under sin.

Sin has taken occasion; it took advantage of the situation. Without the Law, sin (lawlessness) is dead. You can't be a law-breaker without an established law. But is this all the Law was for, to show you your failure? No, the Law was designed to show you the way of life (see **Leviticus 18:5, Deuteronomy 4:1, 30:16, 30:19, Ezekiel 18:9, 20:11, 20:13**). The Law, which was meant to lead people to life, also led some to death because they disobeyed it. The Law, however, remains holy and just and good even while it convicts the sinner by making his sins evident.

Romans 7:15-25

[15] *For what I am doing, I do not understand. For what I will to do, that I do not practice; but what I hate, that I do.* [16] *If, then, I do what I will not to do, I agree with the Law that it is good.* [17] *But now, it is no longer I who do it, but sin that dwells in me.* [18] *For I know that in me (that is, in my flesh) nothing good dwells; for to will is present with me, but how to perform what is good I do not find.* [19] *For the good that I will to do, I do not do; but the evil I will not to do, that I practice.* [20] *Now if I do what I will not to do, it is no longer I who do it, but sin that dwells in me.* [21] *I find then a law, that evil is present with me, the one who wills to do good.* [22] *For I delight in the Law of God according to the inward man.* [23] *But I see another law in my members, warring against the law of my mind, and bringing me into captivity to the law of sin which is in my members.* [24] *O wretched man that I am! Who will deliver me from this body of death?* [25] *I thank God—through Jesus Christ our Lord! So then, with the mind I myself serve the Law of God, but with the flesh the law of sin.*

Paul concludes his thought by expressing a frustrating reality that all God's people can relate to. He truly wants to be obedient to the Law, but he finds something in himself that always conflicts with that desire. There is a *"sin that dwells in [him],"* causing him to do things that he does not want to do! Evil is still present within him, the same individual who loves to do good, and he does not understand it! Paul laments the fact that his sinfulness hampers his obedience. Similar to what Jesus says in **Matthew 26:41**, *"The spirit indeed is willing, but the flesh is weak."* Paul then demonstrates a true heart of gratitude when he expresses his hopelessness to deliver himself from this evil, but his acknowledgment that Jesus Christ has already done so! He ends his thought with the paradox that we all live in. In my mind, I desire to live out the will of God, but in my actions, I continue to fall short.

Romans 8:3 "The Law was Weak Through the Flesh"

³ For what the Law could not do in that it was weak through the flesh, God did by sending His own Son in the likeness of sinful flesh, on account of sin: He condemned sin in the flesh,

Assertion:

The Law is often described as *"weak through the flesh;"* thus, many have determined it to be insignificant and irrelevant.

Response:

As usual, see the context.

³ For what the Law could not do in that it was weak through the flesh, God did by sending His own Son in the likeness of sinful flesh, on account of sin: He condemned sin in the flesh, ⁴ that the righteous requirement of the Law might be fulfilled in us who do not walk according to the flesh but according to the Spirit. ⁵ For those who live according to the flesh set their minds on the things of the flesh, but those who live according to the Spirit, the things of the Spirit. ⁶ For to be carnally minded is death, but to be spiritually minded is life and peace. ⁷ Because the carnal mind is enmity against God; for it is not subject to the Law of God, nor indeed can be. ⁸ So then, those who are in the flesh cannot please God. ³¹

The Law was incapable of fulfilling its intended purpose not because God found fault with it but rather because He found fault with the people themselves. After all, their obedience was not coupled with faith (see **Hebrews 8:8**). Thus, due to their faithlessness, the people prevented the Law from achieving all it was designed to do. The Law cannot be properly done in the flesh and never could be. The Spirit can *only* rightly perform the Law (verse 4). The fleshly mind cannot subject itself to the Law because the flesh is an enemy of God (verse 7).

In the Spirit, however, we are capable and eager to keep the Law of God (see **Ezekiel 36:26-27**) because the Law is spiritual (see **Romans 7:14**), not carnal.

---

[31] Romans 8:3-8

Romans 10:4 "End of the Law"

⁴For Christ is the end of the Law for righteousness to every one who believes.

Assertion:

If Christ is the *"end of the Law,"* then the Law is certainly no longer relevant to one who has faith in Christ, right?

Response:

The word translated as "end" is quite misleading. It's not wrong, but it is not quite right either. When the average reader sees "end" here, they will almost certainly conclude that Christ is the cessation of the Law. The Greek word *can* mean that kind of end, but it also can mean a different kind of end. The Greek word τέλος - Telos means end in the sense of accomplishment, the end goal, the aim, or the point of termination, much in the same way one might speak of the termination of a roadway. It does not mean that the road is made void and needs to be removed; it means that the road has reached its intended goal.

In this context, we can tell that the word τέλος - Telos does not mean the cessation of something but rather the goal of it. Christ is the goal, or aim of the Law, or stated another way, the Law points to, and is perfected in, Christ. Contextually, this makes much more sense because the chapter is about Israel's attempted righteousness.

He says, *"For they (Israel) being ignorant of God's righteousness, and seeking to establish their own righteousness, have not submitted to the righteousness of God. For Christ is the aim of the Law for righteousness to everyone who believes."*

He explains that Israel has been ignorant of God's righteousness (i.e. God's Law, see **Deuteronomy 6:25**) and, therefore, has created their own laws to attain righteousness. This was manifested in the extensive Jewish rulings and traditions in Paul's time. Then Paul explains that Christ is the perfect image of what the Law was trying to accomplish and direct us to. Christ is our perfect example!

The same Greek word (τέλος - Telos) appears in these verses as well. They may make this application of the word a little clearer.

Receiving the end of your faith--the salvation of your souls.[33] We are not being called to *end* our faith but rather to reach the goal of our faith.

"For I say to you that this which is written must still be accomplished in Me: 'And He was numbered with the transgressors.' For the things concerning Me have an end."[34]

"And He was numbered with the transgressors." This is a prophecy from **Isaiah 53:12.** Thus, Jesus explains that this prophecy has a "telos," not a point where the prophecy ceases to be true but rather a point where the prophecy is accomplished.

Now the end of the commandment is charity (love) out of a pure heart, and of a good conscience, and of faith unfeigned. [35]

Does this mean love has *ended* as well? No, love is perfected in the commandment.

Romans 13:8-10 "Love is the Fulfillment of the Law"

[8] Owe no one anything except to love one another, for he who loves another has fulfilled the Law. [9] For the commandments, "You shall not commit adultery," "You shall not murder," "You shall not steal," "You shall not bear false witness," "You shall not covet," and if there is any other commandment, are all summed up in this saying, namely, "You shall love your neighbor as yourself." [10] Love does no harm to a neighbor; therefore love is the fulfillment of the law.

Assertion:
Some have said that the whole Law is just to love one another and nothing more.

---

[32] Romans 10:3-4

[33] *1 Peter 1:9*

[34] *Luke 22:37*

[35] *1 Timothy 1:5 KJV*

Response:

The whole Law, indeed, is to love! However, it is not up to us to define what love is or what it looks like. God gave us guidelines, the details within the Law. These are how God defines loving Himself, one another, and ourselves. Similar to the explanation given in **Matthew 22:37-40,** *[37] Jesus said to him, "'You shall love the LORD your God with all your heart, with all your soul, and with all your mind.' [38] This is the first and great commandment. [39] And the second is like it: 'You shall love your neighbor as yourself.' [40] On these two commandments hang all the Law and the Prophets."*

By God's definition, to love is to do everything He put in His Law. God defines love, not us. Just look at the secular world around us and see how bad we are at determining how to love one another.

Romans 14: "Esteems One Day Above Another / Nothing Unclean of Itself"

(Due to the amount of verses taken from this chapter and the amount of context needed, we will just review the entire chapter piece by piece)

Assertion:

In this chapter, Paul discusses how minor issues such as days observed or food eaten are discerned only by each individual's conscience. The question is, what are these days, and what foods does he address?

Response:

Romans 14:1
[1]Receive one who is weak in the faith, but not to dispute over doubtful things.

Who is Paul talking about? Those who are weak in the faith; the baby believers. He tells us to receive them, even in their weakness. This sentence establishes the context for what follows, and he will continue to explain what this looks like.

Romans 14:2-4

[2] For one believes he may eat all things, but he who is weak eats only vegetables. [3] Let not him who eats despise him who does not eat, and let not him who does not eat judge him who eats; for God has received him. [4] Who are you to judge another's servant? To his own master he stands or falls. Indeed, he will be made to stand, for God is able to make him stand.

Though the chapter never explicitly states what he's discussing, we can make some good guesses based on history. Remember that though this letter was preserved for us, *it was not written to us*. We're listening in on a segment of someone else's conversations. Thus, the author does not need to explain what they were discussing because the audience already knows.

Historically, food sacrificed to idols was a big issue, especially amongst new believers. This is likely the historical context Paul addresses in these first few verses.

This was the letter to the Romans; these Roman converts were all coming out of a pagan system. They grew up sacrificing meat to idols, praying to idols, etc. They attributed power to the idols. They are not likely to just change their minds and think differently overnight. Many of them still attributed power to idols. Because of this, eating meat from an animal sacrificed to an idol - which in their old worldview was an act of worship to that idol - felt like "cheating" on the Lord God.

So when a more mature believer ate meat that may have been offered to an idol, there was a chance that it might cause a new believer to interpret this as an approval of idolatry - thus causing them to stumble in their faith and ascribe power to the idol, and possibly revert to idolatry. Paul also explains this to the Corinthians when he says:

...for some, with consciousness of the idol, until now eat it as a thing offered to an idol; and their conscience, being weak, is defiled. [8]But food does not commend us to God; for neither if we eat are we the better, nor if we do not eat are we the worse. [9]But beware lest somehow this liberty of yours become a stumbling block to those who are weak. [10] For if anyone sees you who have knowledge eating in an idol's temple, will not the conscience of him who is weak be emboldened to eat

those things offered to idols? [11] And because of your knowledge shall the weak brother perish, for whom Christ died? [12] But when you thus sin against the brethren, and wound their weak conscience, you sin against Christ. [13] Therefore, if food makes my brother stumble, I will never again eat meat, lest I make my brother stumble."[36]

In this passage, Paul explains how a weaker brother might see another brother eating food sacrificed to an idol and stumble in their faith, thinking that the example set before them was that they could worship the LORD God *and* their old idols. Let's look at another example of this topic addressed in Corinthians.

[25] Eat whatever is sold in the meat market, asking no questions for conscience' sake; [26] for "the earth is the LORD's, and all its fullness." [27] If any of those who do not believe invites you to dinner, and you desire to go, eat whatever is set before you, asking no question for conscience's sake. [28] But if anyone says to you, "This was offered to idols," do not eat it for the sake of the one who told you, and for conscience' sake; for "the earth is the LORD's, and all its fullness." [29] "Conscience," I say, not your own, but that of the other. For why is my liberty judged by another man's conscience? [30] But if I partake with thanks, why am I evil spoken of for the food over which I give thanks?

Many of the meats sold in the meat markets were first sacrificed to idols. This bothered the new believers, who felt that if they ate the meat, then they were intentionally partaking in the sacrifice to the idol. Paul explains that an idol is nothing, and the meat is still just meat. He also says that if you are told that the meat was sacrificed to idols, not to eat it for the conscience of others to not cause others to think that your new faith in Christ is just another addition to the Greco-Roman Pantheon. Paul wants to clarify that you are no longer part of that old system. You are wholly devoted to Christ. Because of all this, weak believers would then simply abstain from meat altogether, which is why it says, "*he who is weak eats only vegetables.*"[37] Now, switching back to Romans.

---

[36] 1 Corinthians 8:7b-13
1 Corinthians 10:25-30
[37] Romans 14:2

Romans 14:5-6

⁵ One person esteems one day above another, another esteems every day alike. Let each be fully convinced in his own mind. ⁶ He who observes the day, observes it to the Lord; and he who does not observe the day, to the Lord he does not observe it. He who eats, eats to the Lord, for he gives God thanks; and he who does not eat, to the Lord he does not eat, and gives God thanks.

It is often taught that Paul here is teaching about the Sabbath day and that if one desires to keep it, he may, or if not, he doesn't have to. However, the chapter never mentions the Sabbath day (nor does the entire book of Romans).

Here, we move to another topic, but it seems it is still connected to food. The text never specifies exactly what the topic is, just like before, but again, history can be our friend. It seems likely to me that Paul is talking about fasting. Historically, we know that fast days were a huge area of debate in Paul's time, and I'll argue that's what he's addressing (see **Matthew 9:14, Mark 2:18, Luke 5:33, Luke 18:12**). In the Jewish world, it was customary to fast every Monday and Thursday. Some early Christians viewed this as hypocritical and so decreed to fast on Wednesdays and Fridays instead! (see Didache 8:1[38]) Paul says that if one desires to observe a certain day to fast, they can. However, if they choose a different day, or none at all, they can do that too! The Law doesn't say anything about mandatory weekly fasting.

Romans 14:7-9

⁷ For none of us lives to himself, and no one dies to himself. ⁸ For if we live, we live to the Lord; and if we die, we die to the Lord. Therefore, whether we live or die, we are the Lord's. ⁹ For to this end Christ died and rose and lived again, that He might be Lord of both the dead and the living.

---

[38] Didache 8:1 - "But let not your fasts be with the hypocrites, for they fast on the second and fifth day of the week. Rather, fast on the fourth day and the Preparation (Friday)."

Simply, whether you fast or do not fast, eat the meat or do not eat the meat, do it as to the Lord with your best effort and understanding. We should do whatever we do as to the Lord (see **1 Corinthians 10:31**).

Romans 14:10-13

[10] But why do you judge your brother? Or why do you show contempt for your brother? For we shall all stand before the judgment seat of Christ. [11] For it is written:

> *"As I live, says the LORD,*
> *Every knee shall bow to Me,*
> *And every tongue shall confess to God."*

[12] So then each of us shall give account of himself to God. [13] Therefore let us not judge one another anymore, but rather resolve this, not to put a stumbling block or a cause to fall in our brother's way.

He says you should not judge someone else for having a different opinion than you about non-specified theological matters; that is entirely between that individual and God. You are not appointed to determine the nuances of another person's conscience. However, to be clear, something that is specified as a sin in scripture (e.g., "thou shalt not…") must be corrected.

Romans 14:14-18

[14] I know and am convinced by the Lord Jesus that there is nothing unclean of itself; but to him who considers anything to be unclean, to him it is unclean. [15] Yet if your brother is grieved because of your food, you are no longer walking in love. Do not destroy with your food the one for whom Christ died. [16] Therefore do not let your good be spoken of as evil; [17] for the kingdom of God is not eating and drinking, but righteousness and peace and joy in the Holy Spirit. [18] For he who serves Christ in these things is acceptable to God and approved by men.

Is Paul saying that nothing in the entire universe is unclean? If he were, he would be contradicting the rest of scripture. For example, **Leviticus 11** tells us that various animals are unclean to eat. In **Isaiah 6:5**, Isaiah says he is a man of *"unclean lips."* In **Matthew 8:31**, Jesus casts unclean spirits (demons) into unclean animals (pigs). **Revelation 16:13a** says, *"I saw three unclean spirits like frogs…"*

So, if Paul is not trying to rewrite the Bible, what is he saying? I believe he is referring back to the beginning of the chapter. "Clean/unclean" is language that could refer to things sacrificed to idols. One person may deem a piece of biblically clean meat (i.e., beef, lamb, etc) clean no matter what, even if it was offered to Zeus. Another person may deem a piece of meat unclean *because* it was offered to Zeus. Paul considers those who fear consuming such meat *"weak in the faith,"*[39] but nonetheless, he also tells us not to cause them to stumble. Do not let your freedom be a cause of another person's downfall.

Outside of what is stated in the Law, one person may differ from another in their interpretation of what is right or wrong in food or other things. Therefore, *"to him who considers anything to be unclean, to him it is unclean"* - to him, based on his convictions. But to another, it may not be "unclean" because of *his* convictions (see **Romans 14:22-23**). Paul explains that we should not force our convictions on another who sees differently than we do.

In the modern world, for example, some sects of Christianity teach that a woman must wear a long skirt or dress for the sake of modesty, whereas other sects find pants or shorts perfectly acceptable. All that scripture says is that a woman must dress modestly. Although a scriptural standard can be argued, the topic is nonetheless debated, and it can be seen as a "debatable matter." How each person understands modesty will inevitably vary from one to another.

Romans 14:19-23

[19] Therefore let us pursue the things which make for peace and the things by which one may edify another. [20] Do not destroy the work of God for the sake of food. All things indeed are pure, but it is evil for the man who eats with offense. [21] It is good neither to eat meat nor drink wine nor do anything by which your brother stumbles or is offended or is made weak. [22] Do you have faith? Have it to yourself before God. Happy is he who does not condemn himself in what he approves. [23] But he who doubts is condemned if he eats, because he does not eat from faith; for whatever is not from faith is sin.

---

[39] Romans 14:1

Again, Paul teaches not to mislead the weak believers by appearing to eat things sacrificed to idols. We ought to refrain from disputes and divide over things that aren't crystal clear. In Paul's time, whether or not food was sacrificed to an idol. In our time, another comparable example could be churches that teach that things like smoking or drinking are sins, though the bible isn't exactly clear on the subject. Ultimately, you are judged by your convictions, based on your best understanding and honest seeking of God. *"Whatever is not from faith is sin."*

1 Corinthians

1 Corinthians 7:19: "Circumcision is Nothing"

¹⁹ Circumcision is nothing and uncircumcision is nothing, but keeping the commandments of God is what matters.

For more information on defining circumcision, see the entry in **Romans 2:25-29**.

Assertion:

If circumcision is nothing, why would any other of God's commandments be of any importance either?

Response:

People have pointed to Paul's supposed disregard for circumcision (as one of God's commands) as an example, stating that Paul isn't concerned with any of God's Laws. Let's explore this in a historical context:

What does "circumcision" mean to a first-century Jew, such as Paul? When we hear the word "circumcision," we think of a surgical procedure. In the first-century Jewish world, circumcision was much more than a procedure; it was a cultural identifier. To be circumcised, or to be "of the circumcision" is to be a part of the Jewish culture and faith (Consider **Acts 10:45, 11:2, Romans 3:30, 4:9, 4:12, 15:8, Galatians 2:7-9, 2:12, Ephesians 2:11, Philippians 3:3, Colossians**

4:11, Titus 1:10). Thus, Paul brings up both Jew and gentile and says that the distinction is irrelevant before God. What matters, Paul concludes, is the keeping of the commandments of God.

So the irony here is that the very same section that people have used to argue against God's law actually quite emphatically teaches the opposite.

1 Corinthians 10:23 "All Things are Lawful"

All things are lawful for me, but not all things are helpful; all things are lawful for me, but not all things edify.

Assertion:

All things are lawful; I can do whatever I want with freedom in Christ, but the Law still contains "good advice."

Response:

Again, context is key. Keep going to verse 33. [23] *All things are lawful for me, but not all things are helpful; all things are lawful for me, but not all things edify.* [24] *Let no one seek his own, but each one the other's well-being.* [25] *Eat whatever is sold in the meat market, asking no questions for conscience' sake;* [26] *for "the earth is the LORD's, and all its fullness.* [27] *If any of those who do not believe invites you to dinner, and you desire to go, eat whatever is set before you, asking no question for conscience' sake.* [28] *But if anyone says to you, "This was offered to idols," do not eat it for the sake of the one who told you, and for conscience' sake;for "the earth is the Lord's, and all its fullness."* [29] *"Conscience," I say, not your own, but that of the other. For why is my liberty judged by another man's conscience?* [30] *But if I partake with thanks, why am I evil spoken of for the food over which I give thanks?* [31] *Therefore, whether you eat or drink, or whatever you do, do all to the glory of God.* [32] *Give no offense, either to the Jews or to the Greeks or to the church of God,* [33] *just as I also please all men in all things, not seeking my own profit, but the profit of many, that they may be saved.*

Paul is talking about food sacrificed to idols. He explains that these foods are lawful for him to eat (as long as he does not know that they were sacrificed to an idol and are therefore causing another person to stumble; see the entry on **Romans 14**), but they may not be beneficial if they can potentially harm the faith of a weaker believer.

The point is that when we see the world clearly through the eyes of God, then we realize that, as Paul said a couple of chapters earlier, *"An idol is nothing,"*[40] and what God made as good is still good. In this context, the meat of a clean animal that God made for us to consume is still clean, even though the Pagan world has dedicated that clean meat to another god. However, one who does not have that knowledge and still has a *"consciousness of the idol"*[41] regarding it as something to be feared can be confounded by seeing a mature believer partaking in the meat of a pagan sacrifice, thinking that the mature believer is now worshiping numerous gods.

Therefore, all things are lawful to Paul, but not all things are helpful. Paul recognizes this meat sacrificed to an idol as just another piece of meat, disregarding the idol, and acknowledges that not everyone else will see it the way he does. Paul puts much more weight on making sure that the *"weaker brother"*[42] is not misled than he puts on freely enjoying a steak.

If Paul were teaching that *all* things are lawful, then Paul has nothing to teach; we can do whatever is right in our own eyes (see **Deuteronomy 12:8, Judges 17:6, Judges 21:25, Proverbs 21:2**).

1 Corinthians 15:56 "Strength of Sin is Law"

56 The sting of death is sin, and the strength of sin is the Law.

Assertion:

If *"the strength of sin is the Law,"* then the law must be bad, right?

Response:

This is very similar to what Paul explains in **Romans 7:8-11,** *8 But sin, taking opportunity by the commandment, produced in me all manner of evil*

---

[40] 1 Corinthians 8:4

[41] 1 Corinthians 8:7

[42] 1 Corinthians 8:11

desire. For apart from the Law sin was dead. [9] I was alive once without the Law, but when the commandment came, sin revived and I died. [10] And the commandment, which was to bring life, I found to bring death. [11] For sin, taking occasion by the commandment, deceived me, and by it killed me.

Sin has taken "occasion," meaning it took advantage of the situation. Sin (lawlessness, see **1 John 3:4**) is dead without the Law. The Law came, which was meant to lead people to life (see **Leviticus 18:5, Matthew 19:17**), but it also led some to death because they disobeyed it (see **Ezekiel 18:4 and 20**). Therefore, the strength of sin is the Law because, without something to convict of error, there is no standard of right or wrong, and thus, no violation thereof, there is no sin. Simply put, the strength of sin is the Law because the Law creates a standard that can, therefore, be broken. For more on this topic, see the entry on **Romans 7.**

2 Corinthians

2 Corinthians 3:3-18 "Letter kills / Glory Passing Away"

³ clearly you are an epistle of Christ, ministered by us, written not with ink but by the Spirit of the living God, not on tablets of stone but on tablets of flesh, that is, of the heart. ⁴ And we have such trust through Christ toward God. ⁵ Not that we are sufficient of ourselves to think of anything as being from ourselves, but our sufficiency is from God, ⁶ who also made us sufficient as ministers of the new covenant, not of the letter but of the Spirit; for the letter kills, but the Spirit gives life. ⁷ But if the ministry of death, written and engraved on stones, was glorious, so that the children of Israel could not look steadily at the face of Moses because of the glory of his countenance, which glory was passing away, ⁸ how will the ministry of the Spirit not be more glorious? ⁹ For if the ministry of condemnation had glory, the ministry of righteousness exceeds much more in glory. ¹⁰ For even what was made glorious had no glory in this respect, because of the glory that excels. ¹¹ For if what is passing away was glorious, what remains is much more glorious. ¹² Therefore, since we have such hope, we use great boldness of speech —
¹³ unlike Moses, who put a veil over his face so that the children of Israel could not look steadily at the end of what was passing away. ¹⁴ But their minds were blinded. For until this day the same veil remains unlifted in the reading of the Old Testament, because the veil is taken away in Christ. ¹⁵ But even to this day, when Moses is read, a veil lies on their heart. ¹⁶ Nevertheless when one turns to the Lord, the veil is taken away. ¹⁷ Now the Lord is the Spirit; and where the Spirit of the Lord is, there is liberty. ¹⁸ But we all, with unveiled face, beholding as in a mirror the glory of the Lord, are being transformed into the same image from glory to glory, just as by the Spirit of the Lord.

Assertion:

Paul here says that the *"letter kills"* and *"is passing away,"* so many grab onto those phrases and conclude that the Law is abolished.

Response:

The letter Moses administered was glorious, but because it was designed to show us our sin, it only led to the death and condemnation of those who sin. All have sinned (see **Romans 3:23**). The new covenant is more glorious because it is administered by the Spirit in our hearts (see verses **3, 6, 8, 16-17**). The Spirit is given to us so that we may walk in this same covenant that was given to Moses from the inside out, rather than from the outside in (see **Ezekiel 36:26-27**) - from a willful heart and not from external influence (see **Isaiah 29:13**). This is why Paul also says in verses 5 and 6: *"Not that we are sufficient of ourselves to think of anything as being from ourselves, but our sufficiency is from God, who also made us sufficient as ministers of the new covenant, not of the letter but of the Spirit; for the letter kills, but the Spirit gives life."*

Even Moses alludes to the fact that the Law was spiritual and could not be understood in the flesh in **Deuteronomy 29:2-4,** *²Now Moses called all Israel and said to them: "You have seen all that the LORD did before your eyes in the land of Egypt, to Pharaoh and to all his servants and to all his land ³ the great trials which your eyes have seen, the signs, and those great wonders. ⁴ Yet the LORD has not given you a heart to perceive and eyes to see and ears to hear, to this very day.*

Moses tells the multitudes that had personally witnessed the miracles and signs in Egypt and the wilderness that even though they have heard the words of the covenant, God had not yet given them *"a heart to perceive and eyes to see and ears to hear, to this very day."* Pharaoh hardened his own heart to not hear the words of God (see **Exodus 8:32**). God responded by continuing to harden Pharaoh's heart (see **Exodus 9:12**). Likewise, those brought from Egypt refused to hear the words of God (see **Exodus 20:19**) and so God continued this process by further allowing the people's hearts to become hard.

Paul also says in **Romans 8:4-8:** *"...the righteous requirement of the Law might be fulfilled in us who do not walk according to the flesh but according to the Spirit. For those who live according to the flesh set their minds on the things of the flesh, but those who live according to the Spirit, the things of the Spirit. For to be carnally minded is death, but to be spiritually minded is life and peace. Because the carnal mind is enmity against God; for it is not subject to the Law of God, nor indeed can be. So then, those who are in the flesh cannot please God.*

He explains that *only* those walking in the Spirit can "keep the righteous requirement of the Law" because the Law can only properly be observed through the Spirit, not the letter (see **Ezekiel 36:26-27**). The letter kills by bringing condemnation to the guilty, but the Spirit gives life by bringing grace, which enables us to try again to be faithful and obedient. In contrast, however, those who live according to their fleshly mind cannot please God and are, in fact, enemies with Him and are therefore not submitting to His Law.

Galatians

Galatians 2:16 "Not Justified by Law"

[16] *knowing that a man is not justified by the works of the Law but by faith in Jesus Christ, even we have believed in Christ Jesus, that we might be justified by faith in Christ and not by the works of the Law; for by the works of the Law no flesh shall be justified.*

Assertion:

If Law does not justify a man, what purpose is there in observing it?

Response:

The Law alone was *never designed* to be justifying; it is simply a teacher. It was meant to be coupled with faith as manifest evidence of one's belief, as James says: *"You see then that a man is justified by works, and not by faith only"*[43]. Paul and James do not differ in their opinions on this matter (see **Acts 21:18-24**); they simply explain both sides. Paul tells us that James supported the gospel that Paul preached to the Gentiles (see **Galatians 2:9**).

Simply put, if you seek to be justified in God's eyes by observing the Law, you're using the Law for something it was not made to do. It won't work.

---

[43] James 2:24

Galatians 2:19 "Died to the Law"

See **Romans 7**

Galatians 2:21: "If Righteousness is by Law then Christ Died in Vain"

I do not set aside the grace of God; for if righteousness comes through the Law, then Christ died in vain.

Assertion:

Many conclude from this verse that observing the Law would actually be an affront to Christ, insulting his sacrifice.

Response:

Grace and Law are not contrary to each other but rather complimentary. God tells Moses that Moses had found grace in His eyes (see **Exodus 33:12-13**). Was grace a foreign concept to him? No. Moses, the administrator of the Law, prayed to receive this grace as he understood its necessity. So, since Law and grace are not incompatible, we know that Paul is not saying that Law-keepers are acting contrary to God's grace.

Let's turn our attention now to **Deuteronomy 6:25,** which says, *"Then it will be righteousness for us if we are careful to observe all these commandments before the LORD our God, as He has commanded us."* Moses, who wrote this passage, affirms that obedience to God's commandments does yield righteousness for us. Yet, is it mere obedience to the letter that brings us righteousness?

The book of Hebrews speaks of those at Sinai (see **Hebrews 3:16-18** for context). *"For indeed the gospel was preached to us as well as to them [the people at Sinai]; but the word which they heard did not profit them, not being mixed with faith in those who heard it"* [44]

This is why Paul explains that *"Israel, pursuing the Law of righteousness, has not attained to the Law of righteousness. Why? Because they did not seek it by faith, but as it were, by the works of the Law."* [45] Thus, Paul illustrates that righteous deeds alone are not sacrificial, but righteous deeds done out of faith are! This faithful obedience does not make the work of Christ vain.

Galatians 3 "Curse of the Law / No Longer Under a Tutor"

Due to the amount of verses used in this chapter to "prove" the abolition of the Law, we will cover the chapter as a whole. The purpose of this section, however, is still only to explain the questionable verses regarding the Law. This chapter has much treasure that we must gloss over to stay on track.

Assertion:

In this chapter, Paul talks about things like the *"curse of the Law"* and contrasts Law to faith, also describing how the *"Law was our tutor to lead to Christ,"* but *"we are no longer under a tutor,"* thus many have concluded that the Law is bad, and is replaced by faith in Christ. This is understandable, as this chapter is very complex. Let's take some time to get into this subject as we walk through the whole chapter.

Response:
Galatians 3:1-4

[1] *"O foolish Galatians! Who has bewitched you that you should not obey the truth, before whose eyes Jesus Christ was clearly portrayed among you as crucified?* [2] *This only I want to learn from you: Did you receive the Spirit by the works of the Law, or by the hearing of faith?* [3] *Are you so foolish? Having begun in the Spirit, are you now being made perfect by the flesh?* [4] *Have you suffered so many things in vain—if indeed it was in vain?*

---

[44] Hebrews 4:2
[45] Romans 9:31-32

Paul condemns the Galatians for their foolishness because, even though they began this walk by faith alone, they believed the false gospel account of certain Messianic Pharisees who claimed that to be saved, one had to be circumcised and, by implication, become pharisaic (see chapter 2 for context, see **Acts 15** for a similar situation). Paul explains that although it's important to keep the commandments, being motivated by anything other than faithfulness to God results in vain religion that will only ever result in insufficiency. We are saved by faith alone, yet faith without works is dead faith. Does dead faith thus save us? No. A living faith saves us – we are saved when we trust and love God, doing the work that He has commanded out of love and not out of a sense of religious obligation, out of sonship, and not out of slavery/servanthood.

He also stresses that just because a person keeps the commandments, his works do not force God to give him the Spirit, thus making God a debtor (see **Romans 4:4**). Rather, faith comes first and is followed by works. We have an example in Abraham himself: first came faith (see **Genesis 15:6**), and as a result, works came second (see **Genesis 26:5**).

Galatians 3:5

⁵ *"Therefore He who supplies the Spirit to you and works miracles among you, does He do it by the works of the Law, or by the hearing of faith?"*

God, Who sends the Spirit to the saints, works miracles among you. Therefore, does He do these miracles because of your Law obedience, or does He do the miracles because of that spark of trust in your hearts? Does He do miracles among you because you have robotically obeyed the commandments, or has He done miracles because of your love, pursuance, devotion, trust, and faith in Him? God works among you because of your faith! Of course, it's true that if we love God, then we will obey His Law (see **John 14:15, John 14:21-23, John 15:1, 1 John 2:3, 1 John 3:4, 1 John 5:3)**, but faith and love come before works – not the other way around. First comes faith, and then comes works. First, Gentiles learn the basics, and then they are to move on to deeper things (see **Hebrews 6:1-3, Acts 15:19-21).**

Galatians 3:6-9

⁶ *"Just as Abraham believed God, and it was accounted to him for righteousness:* ⁷ *Therefore know that only those who are of faith are sons of Abraham.* ⁸ *And the Scripture, foreseeing that God would justify the Gentiles by faith, preached the gospel to Abraham beforehand, saying, "In you all the nations shall be blessed."* ⁹ *So then those who are of faith are blessed with believing Abraham."*

Abraham trusted and obeyed everything God said, and it was credited to him as righteousness (see **Genesis 15:5-6, Genesis 26:4-5)**. In **Genesis 15:5-6** it says, *"Then He [God] brought him [Abraham] outside and said, "Look now toward heaven, and count the stars if you are able to number them." And He said to him, "So shall your descendants be." And he believed in the LORD, and He accounted it to him for righteousness."* Then, in **Genesis 26:4-5** *"And I will make your descendants multiply as the stars of heaven; I will give to your descendants all these lands; and in your seed all the nations of the earth shall be blessed; because Abraham obeyed My voice and kept My charge, My commandments, My statutes, and My Laws."* Biblically speaking, faith without works is dead – or in other words, there is no such thing as faith without works. However, there are works without faith and these "dead works" are useless because they are not out of love for God. They are, so to speak, intended to make God a debtor, owing the doers of the rewards of the work. However, the Bible is clear that dead works do not save us, and we know that God owes us nothing (see **Romans 4:4-5, Romans 11:35)**. If anything is owed, we owe God a life of continual service done in love and faith (see **Romans 6:12-23, Romans 12:1)**.

Paul uses the phrase *"sons of Abraham"* very intentionally. In the Jewish mind, to be a "son of Abraham" is to be included in the inheritance that Abraham was given, and thus also is culturally viewed as synonymous with being the "chosen people of God" (see **Matthew 3:9, Luke 3:8, 19:9, John 8:39, Romans 9:7-8)**. These people preaching that one must be circumcised, like Abraham, to receive the promise of Abraham are missing the point. Paul points out that it was not the acts of Abraham that merited his favor with God, but it was the faith of Abraham!

Abraham's faith was accounted to him for righteousness: Therefore, be aware that those of faith are sons of Abraham, and thus, heirs to the covenants of promise (see **Galatians 3:29, Ephesians 2:11-13**). God preached the Gospel to Abraham beforehand, saying, *"In you all the nations shall be blessed."* It was foretold in scripture that God would justify the Gentiles by faith; therefore, those who are of faith are blessed by believing like Abraham.

Galatians 3:10

[10] *"For as many as are of the works of the Law are under the curse; for it is written, "Cursed is everyone who does not continue in all things which are written in the book of the Law, to do them."*

Those who are in covenant with God are under a curse. What do I mean? Part of God's covenant through Moses is **Deuteronomy 28**, called the blessings and the curses. There is a blessing to obey the Law and a curse (a punishment, a penalty) not to obey the Law. But *"all have sinned"*[46], and are thus all under the curse, to some extent or another. So we're all cursed? Yes, actually, but there is good news. But we'll have to keep reading to find out more.

It is written, [26] *"Behold, I set before you today a blessing and a curse: [27] the blessing, if you obey the commandments of the LORD your God which I command you today; [28] and the curse, if you do not obey the commandments of the LORD your God* [47](see also **Deuteronomy 27:15-26, 30:1, 30:15, 30:19**)

So, according to the Law, the curse of the Law is not obeying the Law! Paul never said that the Law is a curse. He said that there is a curse in the Law!

Galatians 3:11-12

[11] *"But that no one is justified by the Law in the sight of God is evident, for "the just shall live by faith."* [12] *Yet the Law is not of faith, but "the man who does them shall live by them."*

---

[46] Romans 3:23

[47] Deuteronomy 11:26-28a

The Law justifies no one; no one was ever expected to. The Law distinguishes right from wrong and administers judgment as needed. But God was not surprised to see that *"all have sinned and fall short of the glory of God"*[48]. No one can be sinless. Fortunately, God has made it clear in scripture that he wasn't looking for that. He was looking for a faithful[49] heart, which, despite being marred by a sinful nature, loved Him and served Him as best as they possibly could. For example, look to David, the murderous, adulterating man after God's own heart. God was pleased with David's attitude of repentance far more than He was bothered by David's momentary failures.

Galatians 3:13-14

[13] *"Christ has redeemed us from the curse of the Law, having become a curse for us. For it is written, "Cursed is everyone who hangs on a tree,"* [14] *that the blessing of Abraham might come upon the Gentiles in Christ Jesus, that we might receive the promise of the Spirit through faith."*

Christ has saved us from having to receive the curse mentioned in the Law — that is, the death penalty one would deserve for breaking the Law (see **Deuteronomy 28**). Christ has saved us from having to receive that death penalty, instead taking it on himself and thus paying our debt. We owed God our lives when we sinned, yet Christ offered his life to God so that we would not have to pay our own debt at the cost of our lives!

God wanted the promise to Abraham to come to pass as magnificently as possible, not for Abraham's sake, but for His own sake. God is seeking to invite all people to Himself. It was Israel's job from the beginning of its formation as a nation. God says to the newly formed nation, *"You shall be to Me a kingdom of priests and a holy nation."*, A priest's job is to intercede for other people, but if the whole kingdom is meant to be interceding on behalf of another, who is the "other"? It's the rest of the world!

---

[48] Romans 3:23, Genesis 12:3b, Exodus 19:6a

[49] When the Old Testament uses the word "faith," (אמון /אמונה , emun/ emunah) it would more accurately be rendered as faithful or faithfulness.

God sent His Son into the world to redeem those who walk in faithfulness, despite the fact they *even* have fallen short of God's righteous standard, to spread His message *"in Jerusalem, and in all Judaea and Samaria, and to the ends of the earth"!*[50] It's all about Him! See what God says to Isaiah:

"Hear this, O house of Jacob, who are called by the name of Israel...For My name's sake, I will defer My anger, And [for] My praise I will restrain it from you, So that I do not cut you off. Behold, I have refined you, but not as silver; I have tested you in the furnace of affliction. For My own sake, for My own sake, I will do [it;] For how should [My name] be profaned? [51]

Galatians 3:15-18

[15] *"Brethren, I speak in the manner of men: Though it is only a man's covenant,* yet if it is confirmed, no one annuls or adds to it. [16] *Now to Abraham and his Seed were the promises made. He does not say, "And to seeds," as of many, but as of one, "And to your Seed," who is Christ.* [17] *And this I say, that the Law, which was four hundred and thirty years later, cannot annul the covenant that was confirmed before by God in Christ, that it should make the promise of no effect.* [18] *For if the inheritance is of the Law, it is no longer of promise; but God gave it to Abraham by promise."*

He speaks like a man, like an average guy speaking frankly. If both parties involved agree upon a human contract (whether in business, marriage, etc.), then no one can add more words to the contract, and no one can take away words from it. Simply put, God made a covenant with Abraham, and even though God also made a covenant through Moses, that cannot change the terms of the covenant already made to Abraham.

God made a promise to both Abraham and his seed. God made this promise to Abraham's "seed" (singular), not "seeds" (plural). God

---

[50] Acts 1:8, see also Matthew 28:19, Mark 16:15

[51] Isaiah 48:1a, 9-11a

made a promise to Abraham and *one* seed, and that "seed" is Jesus. The predetermined plan for Christ to come and fulfill what God had intended through the terms of His covenant with Abraham cannot be interrupted. It had to happen; even if another covenant had to be made in the meantime, it could not change the effectuality of the Abrahamic covenant. Thus, we can also see that even though the Mosaic covenant has been ratified, God's ultimate covenant promise of the inheritance made to Abraham (see **Genesis 15:18**) cannot be altered.

The Sinai Covenant neither ruined nor altered the Abrahamic Covenant because the two covenants, though complimenting each other, were not dependent on one another. When a new covenant was made in the bible, it did not annul the former but existed beside it. In **Ephesians 2:12,** Paul discusses the covenants of promise (plural). God's covenant with Noah to not flood the world again was not annulled when He made a covenant with Abraham, right?

Galatians 3:19-20

[19] *"What purpose then does the Law serve? It was added because of transgressions, till the Seed should come to whom the promise was made; and it was appointed through messengers[52] by the hand of a mediator.* [20] *Now a mediator does not mediate for one only, but God is one."*

So then, why did God even give the Law to us? He gave it because of our sinfulness. Because we were so corrupt, God had to point out our errors and correct us. If it wasn't for the Law, people would never have learned what "sin" is (see **Romans 7:7**), and thus we would have kept on sinning. So, in this sense, the Law was a blessing because it teaches us what sin is, and with this knowledge, we can learn what is good and what is bad in the eyes of God and ultimately catch a glimpse of the heart of God. However, although we then learned what we should and should not do, what righteousness is, and what sin is, we did

---

52 I have edited the NKJV in this passage. "Messengers" here is the Greek word "ἄγγελος / aggelos." The Hebrew word is "מַלְאָךְ / malakh." These words both mean messenger, yet are often translated as "angel." They can refer to both a human messenger and a heavenly one. This is why many translations say "appointed through angels." However, I believe that Young's Literal Translation is correct in translating this word as simply "messenger" rather than specifically "angel" (which in modern English has the connotation of a divine being).

not yet have a good example of how to implement those things.

For example, how do we love our neighbor when the Law says, *"You shall love your neighbor?"* [53] How are we to act justly when the Bible says, *"act justly"* [54]? How are we to observe the Sabbath when the Bible says to keep it holy and do no work (see **Exodus 20:8-11**)? The Law was all we had to teach us about what is right and what is wrong. We were left to figure out how to implement it – and we often got it wrong. We were left with only the Law until the "seed" - Christ came to show us how to properly apply it (see **Matthew 5:17**).

So, simply put, the Law was given by God until the "seed" would arrive. This does not mean that the Law was only authoritative until Jesus arrived; it simply means that it was all we had to teach us about right and wrong until Jesus came. Now, the commandments were given by means of messengers. "Messengers" carry the message regarding the covenant throughout the Bible. I would attribute this word to prophets, scribes, and the like. The prime messenger, Moses, was also a mediator between the one God and the Israelites at Sinai.

So, in short, why did God give us the Law? We kept sinning, and we needed the Law to show us how we were sinning because the Law itself defines sin (see **1 John 3:4**). The Law was appointed by messengers and through a mediator, Moses, who mediated between God and man.

Galatians 3:21

[21] *"Is the Law then against the promises of God? Certainly not! For if there had been a law given which could have given life, truly righteousness would have been by the Law."*

Is the Law against God's promises (including the promise of the new covenant)? Certainly not! For if it were possible that a law could be given that could have given life instead of the death penalty curse, then surely righteousness would have been by that law.

---

[53] Leviticus 19:18

[54] Micah 6:8

Does this mean that the Law does not give life? On the contrary, God says, *"Every commandment which I command you today you must be careful to observe, that you may live and multiply, and go in and possess the land of which the LORD swore to your fathers"*[55]. As the Law says, we shall surely live if we obey and to the proportionate measure in which we obey. However, no one has kept the Law perfectly except Jesus (see **Hebrews 4:14-15**). Therefore, we all deserve to die (see **Deuteronomy 28, Romans 3:23, Hebrews 10:28**). Although this Law was designed to give us life, sin took advantage of the Law, and instead, the Law was forced to give us death (see **Romans 7:10-15**).

We have all fallen short of God's perfect standard except Jesus Christ. This is why it is so important that we recognize what God has done through Jesus. Because of Christ's perfection, God could raise him from the dead and make him the perfect sacrifice for our sins (see **Hebrews 10:14-18**). The perfect Law-keeper died for the imperfect Law-breakers! We must inherit the righteousness of the perfect one, Jesus.

Galatians 3:22

[22] *"But the Scripture has confined all under sin, that the promise by faith in Jesus Christ might be given to those who believe."*

But scripture, particularly the Law, has acted as a judge and determined that everyone is a transgressor. It convicts us of wrongdoing and preordains our punishment—the cursed death penalty. Therefore, by faith in Jesus Christ, the promise made to Abraham might be extended to all those who believe (see **Romans 11, Galatians 3:28-29).** Christ came and did what he did so that those who are faithful to him might be grafted into the Abrahamic Covenant.

Galatians 3:23-25:

[23] *"But before faith came, we were kept under guard by the Law, kept for the faith which would afterward be revealed.* [24]*Therefore the Law was our tutor to bring us to Christ, that we might be justified by faith.* [25]*But after faith has come, we are no longer under a tutor."*

---

[55] Deuteronomy 8:1

παιδαγωγός / Paidagogos (pron. "pay-dah-gah-gowss") is usually translated as "tutor" or "schoolmaster" – two poor translations. However, no better English alternatives are available since no exact English equivalent exists. Paidagogos (Strong's G3807) means "child-conductor," a teacher of children, also used for slaves, those who are not mature. Strong's Lexicon defines it this way:

"A tutor, i.e., a guardian and guide of boys. Among the Greeks and the Romans, the name was applied to trustworthy slaves charged with supervising the lives and morals of boys belonging to the better class. The boys were not allowed to step out of the house without them before they reached manhood."

We were under the tutor (paidagogos) until Christ because we were spiritually young children (Gk. παῖς / pais).

This word is used only one other time in the New Testament in **1 Corinthians 4:15-21**. *For though you might have ten thousand child-conductors in Christ, yet you do not have many fathers; for in Christ Jesus I have begotten you through the gospel. Therefore I urge you, imitate me. For this reason I have sent Timothy to you, who is my beloved and faithful son in the Lord, who will remind you of my ways in Christ, as I teach everywhere in every church. Now some are puffed up, as though I were not coming to you. But I will come to you shortly, if the Lord wills, and I will know, not the word of those who are puffed up, but the power. For the kingdom of God is not in word but in power. What do you want? Shall I come to you with a rod, or in love and a spirit of gentleness?"* Paul says there are many who will conduct you as if you were children or slaves. But few who will father you with love. He then says, "shall I come to you with the rod or in love?" Paul compares the child conductors - and thus the Law - to a rod, a disciplinarian designed to keep us in line. We are no longer under this disciplinarian; we are under the love of the Father. Has the instruction changed? No, but the means of delivering it has.

Before God sent His Son to lead us to faith (see **Hebrews 12:2**), a *paidagogos* had kept watch over us; that *paidagogos,* which guarded us and kept watch over us, was the Law. The Law kept watch over us as a collective people in our stage of immaturity until the time when the faith that would be revealed by Christ would come. Therefore, the Law was our *paidagogos* to lead us to maturity—to be like Christ.

This was the job of the Law: to train us in the way we should go so that when we arrived at the appointed age of maturity, we could be delivered from the punishment-power of the Law and delivered into the love of the Father. A father may discipline a young child, but when the child has become an adult, the relationship changes, and the parent does not try to discipline like they used to anymore. That stage has passed, and the child has matured into adulthood.

A *paidagogos* is like the picture of the stereotypical (or imagined) British nanny. She raises the children, teaches them right from wrong, punishes them when they disobey and cares for their needs. However, her ultimate goal is to guide the children to the point where they can one day provide for themselves, correct themselves, and make themselves do right and avoid wrong. Although she will no longer be needed when the children reach maturity, the rules, guidance, wisdom, etc., she gave them will not be done away with. Similarly, the curse of the Law (i.e., the punishment of the nanny is now fulfilled, completed, and no longer in effect because Christ paid our debt (which we acquired by sinning)

Just as the nanny leaves the children and the children live their lives based on the guidance, wisdom, and rules of the nanny, we likewise must mature beyond the former covenant (the one which punished us with a death-penalty-curse) and grow into the new covenant (one where we can now worship in spirit and truth, living according to the guidance of the Law, led by the Spirit), (see **Ezekiel 36:26-27**) and being forgiven by Christ when we occasionally transgress. Just as it ought to be our ambition to live by the way our nanny taught us, we likewise should live by the way the Law taught us.

Now that we have received the "faith of Abraham" through Jesus (see **Romans 4:16-25)**, we are no longer under the disciplinarian who guides us (i.e., Law (see **Romans 8:1**)). Has the instruction changed? No, since the intention was that we would be trained in the Law since our youth and be prepared for when the Messiah would come.

The Law was our "paidagogos," our child conductor or nanny, designed to direct us toward Christ. It can no longer punish (see **Romans 8:1, Galatians 3:13)** because we are no longer children. We are supposed to be spiritual adults, living by the Spirit, with the Law written on our hearts, in our innermost being, as we were taught from a "young age" (see **Ezekiel 36:26-27, Jeremiah 31:33.**) Therefore, walk and live spiritually mature.

(Note: "paidagogos" is somewhat further explained as Paul continues to preach in **Galatians 4:1-7.**)

Galatians 3:26-29

[26] *"For you are all sons of God through faith in Christ Jesus.* [25] *For as many of you as were baptized into Christ have put on Christ.* [28] *There is neither Jew nor Greek, there is neither slave nor free, there is neither male nor female; for you are all one in Christ Jesus.* [29] *And if you are Christ's, then you are Abraham's seed, and heirs according to the promise.*

If you have Abraham-like faith in Christ Jesus, then you are all sons of God. *For as many of you as were baptized into Christ have put on Christ,* meaning to say, you live like Christ, mature and obedient to the will of the Father. There is neither Jew nor Greek (see **Exodus 12:49, Leviticus 24:22, Numbers 15:15-16, Numbers 15:29)** regarding salvation. Both are saved by the same means – faith (see **Romans 3:28-31)**. Likewise, there is no difference in terms of salvation between men and women or freedmen and those in slavery. Regardless of who you are or where you come from, anyone can be saved if they are faithful to the God of Abraham and His promised "seed." If a person has Abraham-like faith, then the person will be numbered among Abraham's descendants and thus also heirs according to the promise.

Galatians 4:8-11 "You Observe Days and Months and Seasons and Years"

⁸ But then, indeed, when you did not know God, you served those which by nature are not gods. ⁹ But now after you have known God, or rather are known by God, how is it that you turn again to the weak and beggarly elements, to which you desire again to be in bondage? ¹⁰ You observe days and months and seasons and years. ¹¹ I am afraid for you, lest I have labored for you in vain.

Assertion:

Paul talks about being afraid for the Galatians, who *"observe days and months and seasons and years."* Many have assumed that Paul is speaking of God's holy days and then conclude that Paul is teaching against their observance as if it were contrary to faith in Christ. Let's explore.

Response:

It is often said that the days, months, seasons, and years, as well as the weak and beggarly elements Paul refers to, are God's holy days, especially the Sabbath. The key here is verse 8. *"When you did not know God, you served those which by nature are not gods."* Paul is speaking of the things they observed while they were pagans!

It is important to realize that pagan religions also had holy days. Many of those same ancient Greco-Roman holy days that Paul was specifically speaking of have morphed into our own culture's holidays (for example, Christmas, Easter, Valentine's Day, Halloween, New Year, etc.). Paul is referring to the pagan days when he speaks of those who are *"not gods"* when *"you did not know God."*

Galatians 4:21-31 "Cast out the Bondwoman and Her Son"

²¹ Tell me, you who desire to be under the Law, do you not hear the Law? ²² For it is written that Abraham had two sons: the one by a bondwoman, the other by a freewoman. ²³ But he who was of the bondwoman was born according to the flesh, and he of the freewoman through promise, ²⁴ which things are symbolic. For these are the two covenants: the one from Mount Sinai which gives birth to bondage, which is Hagar— ²⁵ for this Hagar is Mount Sinai in Arabia and corresponds to

Jerusalem which now is, and is in bondage with her children — ²⁶ , *but the Jerusalem above is free, which is the mother of us all. For it is written:*
"Rejoice, O barren,
You who do not bear!
Break forth and shout,
You who are not in labor!
For the desolate has many more children
Than she who has a husband."

²⁸ *Now we, brethren, as Isaac was, are children of promise.* ²⁹ *But, as he who was born according to the flesh then persecuted him who was born according to the Spirit, even so it is now.* ³⁰ *Nevertheless what does the Scripture say? "Cast out the bondwoman and her son, for the son of the bondwoman shall not be heir with the son of the freewoman."* ³¹ *So then, brethren, we are not children of the bondwoman but of the free.*

Assertion:

It has been said simply that Mt. Sinai is bondage that must be cast off, which is all this section tells us. I propose that that is a gross misunderstanding of this section. Let's get into it and see what Paul is telling us:

Response:

Verses 21-24: The "promise" was the promise that God gave to Abraham – firstly, that his descendants should be more numerous than the sand of the seashore and more numerous than all the countable stars in the sky. Secondly, those innumerable descendants would inherit the promised land (see **Genesis 15:5, 18-21**); Abraham, however, after many years of not seeing this promise come to pass, began to feel that he needed to help the Almighty out. He, through Hagar, conceived Ishmael and asked that God would accept him (see **Genesis 17:18-19**). But God had not forgotten His promise and intended to carry it out as planned. Here, we see a contrast: there is one path to the promises of God through human effort and one through divine effort. These things are symbolic.

Verses 25-27: This Hagar, this human effort towards God's promises, is comparable to Mt. Sinai, which is in Arabia, in the desert, outside the land of promise. It "gives birth to bondage," to bind you by obligation, manifest in Paul's day by the present condition of the physical city of

Jerusalem, in bondage by a religious system, and lacking the freedom of the promise. This represents those who attempt to earn their favor with God by ritual observance and fail to walk faithfully with God. Thus, *"The desolate has many more children than she who has a husband."* In contrast, the "Jerusalem above," the "promised land" from heaven, is free. It relies entirely on God's faithfulness and not at all on human effort.

Verses 28-31: Paul admonishes his hearers to be like Isaac was, children of promise, following God by faithful obedience, rather than trying to "help Him" fulfill His promise. Paul also acknowledges that the spiritual "Ishmael" will always be there to persecute spiritual "Isaac." *Nevertheless, what does the Scripture say? "Cast out the bondwoman and her son, for the son of the bondwoman shall not be heir with the son of the freewoman."* Spiritual "Ishmael" will not inherit the kingdom of God; they will be cast out. Stay firm in your faith.

Galatians 5:6 "Neither Circumcision nor Uncircumcision"

⁶ For in Christ Jesus neither circumcision nor uncircumcision avails anything, but faith working through love.

Assertion:

If circumcision does not avail anything, why would any other of God's commandments be of any value either?

Response:

Here, we see three more verses that generally say the same thing:

"For in Christ Jesus neither circumcision nor uncircumcision avails anything, but a new creation [avails]." [56]

"Circumcision is nothing and uncircumcision is nothing, but keeping the commandments of God is what matters."

---

[56] Galatians 6:15, 1 Corinthians 7:19

"25 For circumcision is indeed profitable if you keep the Law; but if you are a breaker of the Law, your circumcision has become uncircumcision. 26 Therefore, if an uncircumcised man keeps the righteous requirements of the Law, will not his uncircumcision be counted as circumcision? 27 And will not the physically uncircumcised, if he fulfills the Law, judge you who, even with your written code and circumcision, are a transgressor of the Law? 57

It is important to understand that when the New Testament speaks of "the" circumcision, it is not speaking of the act of circumcision but rather speaks of Judaism or sometimes ethnic Jews in general. (see **Acts 10:45, 11:2, Romans 3:30, 4:9, 4:12, 15:8, Galatians 2:7-9, 2:12, Ephesians 2:11, Philippians 3:3, Colossians 4:11, Titus 1:10)**. Thus, this is comparable to when Paul says, *"There is neither Jew nor Greek"* in God's eyes (see **Galatians 3:28, Colossians 3:11)**. His point is that God makes no genealogical distinctions between His people, God does not play favorites.

So what we can understand from all these verses mentioning the same concept: circumcision is nothing and uncircumcision is nothing, but faith working through love avails because it makes us a new creation, one capable of keeping the commandments. It doesn't matter if you're ethnically Jewish, if you're an ethnically Gentile convert to Judaism, or just a God-fearing Gentile; if you're walking in obedience and faithfulness to God, being "of the circumcision" doesn't matter.

There was a belief among many Jews that God-fearing Gentiles were inferior to ethnic Jews and Gentile converts to Judaism. Thus, a "Court of the Gentiles" (not commanded by God) existed, which was part of the Temple complex that Herod had built. Only Jews were allowed into the Temple itself, while Gentiles were excluded from entering –being restricted to the court outside the actual Temple. This was a rule instituted by Herod **(see Josephus, War of the Jews 5.5.2.193-199)**. That courtyard was as close to the Temple, and thus, the presence of God as a faithful, God-fearing Gentile could get in their culture. Paul is arguing that even if the culture says that a gentile is a second-class believer, in

---

57 Romans 2:25-27

God's eyes, it doesn't matter whether a person is "of the circumcision" or not. If you faithfully keep the covenant, that's all that counts. God-fearing Gentiles *are allowed by God* to come into the Temple to worship (see **Isaiah 56:6-7**). These commandment-keeping God-fearers will even judge those Jews who do not have faith in Jesus (see **Romans 2:27**).

Galatians 5:18 "Not Under the Law"
18But if you are led by the Spirit, you are not under the Law.

Assertion:
Many people read this as saying, "If you follow the Spirit, you cannot follow the Law."

Response:
Context is always key.

16 I say then: Walk in the Spirit, and you shall not fulfill the lust of the flesh. 17 For the flesh lusts against the Spirit, and the Spirit against the flesh; and these are contrary to one another so that you do not do the things that you wish. 18 But if you are led by the Spirit, you are not under the Law. 19 Now the works of the flesh are evident, which are: adultery, fornication, uncleanness, lewdness, 20 idolatry, sorcery, hatred, contentions, jealousies, outbursts of wrath, selfish ambitions, dissensions, heresies, 21 envy, murders, drunkenness, revelries, and the like; of which I tell you beforehand, just as I also told you in time past, that those who practice such things will not inherit the kingdom of God. 22 But the fruit of the Spirit is love, joy, peace, longsuffering, kindness, goodness, faithfulness, 23 gentleness, self-control. Against such there is no law. 58

If you walk in the Spirit, you will not fulfill the lusts of the flesh. The lusts of the flesh, as listed below, are all defined in the Law as sin. To be "under the Law" is to be under the bondage of sin and its corresponding punishments. According to **Deuteronomy 28,** to be under the Law is to be under the curse of the Law. On the other hand, having the fruit of the Spirit is the opposite of the curse (fruit of

---

58 Galatians 5:16-23

disobedience). To have the Spirit is to walk in obedience (see **Ezekiel 36:26-27**; thus, it is not against any law!

Galatians 6:15 "Neither Circumcision nor Uncircumcision"

Please see **Galatians 5:6**

Ephesians

Ephesians 2:14-18 "Having abolished the Law of Commandments"

^{14} For He Himself is our peace, who has made both one, and has broken down the middle wall of separation, ^{15} having abolished in His flesh the enmity, that is, the law of commandments contained in ordinances, so as to create in Himself one new man from the two, thus making peace, ^{16} and that He might reconcile them both to God in one body through the cross, thereby putting to death the enmity. $_{17}$ And He came and preached peace to you who were afar off and to those who were near. ^{18} For through Him we both have access by one Spirit to the Father.

Assertion:

Christ abolished the "Law of commandments!" Paul must be speaking of the Mosaic Law, right?

Response:

People will often quote, *"He abolished the law of commandments contained in ordinances,"* removing it from its context and stating that Christ abolished God's Law, generally ignoring the rest of the section. This is truly a shame; this section in context is utterly amazing. So, what exactly is Paul talking about? He's talking about Ezekiel's two-stick prophecy.

Israel was once a single, united kingdom divided into the Northern House of Israel and the Southern House of Judah. The northern house of Israel was dispersed among the nations and lost. Ezekiel prophecies this lost house will be found, and the two houses will become *"one stick in your hand"* again. Ezekiel says this:

15 Again the word of the LORD came to me, saying, 16 "As for you, son of man, take a stick for yourself and write on it: 'For Judah and for the children of Israel, his companions.' Then take another stick and write on it, 'For Joseph, the stick of Ephraim, and for all the house of Israel, his companions.' 17 Then join them one to another for yourself into one stick, and they will become one in your hand. 18 "And when the children of your people speak to you, saying, 'Will you not show us what you mean by these?'— 19 say to them, 'Thus says the Lord GOD: "Surely I will take the stick of Joseph, which is in the hand of Ephraim, and the tribes of Israel, his companions; and I will join them with it, with the stick of Judah, and make them one stick, and they will be one in My hand." ' 20 And the sticks on which you write will be in your hand before their eyes. 21 "Then say to them, 'Thus says the Lord GOD: "Surely I will take the children of Israel from among the nations, wherever they have gone, and will gather them from every side and bring them into their own land; 22 and I will make them one nation in the land, on the mountains of Israel; and one king shall be king over them all; they shall no longer be two nations, nor shall they ever be divided into two kingdoms again. 23 They shall not defile themselves anymore with their idols, nor with their detestable things, nor with any of their transgressions; but I will deliver them from all their dwelling places in which they have sinned, and will cleanse them. Then they shall be My people, and I will be their God. 24 "David My servant shall be king over them, and they shall all have one shepherd; they shall also walk in My judgments and observe My statutes, and do them. 25 Then they shall dwell in the land that I have given to Jacob My servant, where your fathers dwelt; and they shall dwell there, they, their children, and their children's children, forever; and My servant David shall be their prince forever. 26 Moreover I will make a covenant of peace with them, and it shall be an everlasting covenant with them; I will establish them and multiply them, and I will set My sanctuary in their midst forevermore. 27 My tabernacle also shall be with them; indeed I will be their God, and they shall be My people. 28 The nations also will know that I, the LORD, sanctify Israel, when My sanctuary is in their midst forevermore.""

So what is "the law of commandments contained in ordinances?" It was the man-made commandments of mainstream Judaism that declared the Gentiles to be unclean (as in **Acts 10** and **11**) that kept the tribe of Judah apart from the other tribes dispersed amongst the nations. In Paul's time, this was manifest by a literal, physical "middle wall of separation" called the "soreg"[60] which was in place to keep non-Jews away from the Temple. Jesus came to abolish this law, to break down this barrier, so that all the tribes of Israel can, and will, be reunited into one "stick" again, with David (metaphorically speaking of Jesus) as their king.

The Greek word translated "ordinances" in this section is "δόγμα, dógma," which means "decree," and the root word of "dógma" is "δοκέω, dokéō." It means to suppose (what "seems to be"), forming an opinion (a personal judgment, estimate). According to Strong's Greek Lexicon, "suppose" (dokéō) directly reflects the personal perspective (values) of the person making the subjective judgment call, i.e., showing what they esteem (or do not esteem) as an individual. Both "dokéō" and "dógma" stress "the subjective mental estimate or opinion about a matter."

Are the commandments contained within the Mosaic Law "subjective mental estimates or opinions"? No! They are directly from God, often beginning with "Thus says the LORD..." (also see **Ezra 7:6, 7:12**) and are not the inventions of opinionated legislators or lawyers - the "dokéō" and "dógma" are the traditions and doctrines of man that have created this artificial distinction between Jew and gentile. They are contrary to God's Law!

---

[59] Ezekiel 37:21-28

[60] described in Josephus Wars of the Jews, Book 5, Chapter 5, Section 2; also found in archeology

Colossians 2:14-15 "Wiped out the Handwriting of Requirements"

¹⁴ *having wiped out the handwriting of requirements that were against us, which was contrary to us. And He has taken it out of the way, having nailed it to the cross.* ¹⁵ *Having disarmed principalities and powers, He made a public spectacle of them, triumphing over them in it.*

Assertion:

Jesus wiped out the handwriting of requirements, which *must* refer to the Old Testament Law, right? Maybe not. Let's examine.

Response:

The "handwriting of requirements" is the point in question. "Handwriting" comes from the Greek "χειρόγραφον, cheirographon" meaning exactly that, something written by one's hand, which would imply it was written of their own will.

"Requirements" comes from the Greek "δόγμα, dogma" which means "decree" and the root word of "dógma" is "δοκέω, dokéō" meaning suppose (what "seems to be"), forming an opinion (a personal judgment, estimate). According to Strong's Greek Lexicon, "suppose" (dokéō) directly reflects the personal perspective (values) of the person making the subjective judgment call, i.e., showing what they esteem (or do not esteem) as an individual. Both "dokéō" and "dógma" stress "the subjective mental estimate or opinion about a matter."

With all this information, we can summarize that the "handwriting of requirements" is about those man-made rulings of Judaism that are contrary to the Law of God, and the principle would apply to all man-made religious decrees, including those of the Christian religion. Christ set us free from human-decreed religion (see **Matthew 23:8-10**). By Christ, we can serve the Father through one and only one mediator - Christ himself! (see **1 Timothy 2:5**).

Colossians 2:16-19 "Let No One Judge You"

[16] So let no one judge you in food or in drink, or regarding a festival or a new moon or sabbaths, [17] which are a shadow of things to come, but the substance is of Christ. [18] Let no one cheat you of your reward, taking delight in false humility and worship of angels, intruding into those things which he has not seen, vainly puffed up by his fleshly mind, [19] and not holding fast to the Head, from whom all the body, nourished and knit together by joints and ligaments, grows with the increase that is from God.

Assertion:

When it says, *"let no one judge you..."* in these things, it is usually taken to mean that we ought not to judge another believer for not doing them, implying that we don't need to be doing them anyway.

Response:

Contextually, it may better be understood as "Let no *unbeliever* judge you..." Let's look at the context leading up to this statement. We see phrases like *Beware lest anyone cheat you through philosophy and empty deceit, according to the tradition of men, according to the basic principles of the world, and not according to Christ.* [61], and *having wiped out the handwriting of requirements that were against us, which was contrary to us.* When we see the subject of the chapter as a whole, it becomes quite evident that the topic being discussed is a human-created religion, whether it be pagan or Jewish. Paul instructs his hearers not to let *these people* judge you because you *are* observing these things!

---

[61] Colossians 2:8, Colossians 2:14a

Pagans would look down upon you for the same reasons a modern person would look down on you; it's just foreign and weird to them and doesn't make sense. Jews would look down upon you because their man-made decrees state that to observe such things, you must first become a full-fledged Jew (i.e., circumcised), and much of Paul's audience has not been.

As we progress, the context further reinforces that we're talking about unbelievers, as it says that they are *"taking delight in false humility and worship of angels, intruding into those things which he has not seen, vainly puffed up by his fleshly mind, and not holding fast to the Head (Christ)".*

Verse 17 in the NKJV says, *"But the substance is of Christ."* Many translations sound very similar. However, the word "substance" more literally is "body," and the word "is" isn't in Greek but rather is an interpreter's decision. Another way to render this passage might read: *"But the body of Christ."* In context, it would then read: *"So let no one judge you in food or in drink, or regarding a festival or a new moon or sabbaths, which are a shadow of things to come, but the body of Christ."* The body of Christ is the only people that should judge each other regarding the details of such things (see also **1 Corinthians 5:12-13**)! Additionally, we know that the body of Christ was observing these feasts: Passover, Unleavened Bread, Day of Trumpets (a.k.a. Pentecost), Day of Atonement, Tabernacles (see **Leviticus 23**) Some examples of early believers observing the feasts are **Acts 2:1-21, 18:21, 20:6, 20:16, 1 Corinthians 5:6-8, 16:8.**

Lastly, it must be understood that shadows aren't bad things. When Paul writes about these things as *"a shadow of things to come,"* he does not intend to degrade them. The sabbaths, festivals, and many other "ritual" commandments are prophetic pictures of things to be fulfilled in Christ. Thus, they are Christ's shadow. They bear a resemblance to him, but they are not his actual substance.

Looking at the shadow of someone can tell us two things. Firstly, we can get an idea of what they look like, albeit not very clearly. Secondly, we can tell they are near, for a shadow never appears apart from its source. By observing these commandments, they will quickly point us to Christ. However, this fact does not nullify them but adds a fuller depth to them. See how Paul views the Passover in light of Christ. *⁷Therefore purge out the old leaven, that you may be a new lump, since you truly are unleavened. For indeed Christ, our Passover, was sacrificed for us. ⁸Therefore let us keep the feast, not with old leaven, nor with the leaven of malice and wickedness, but with the unleavened [bread] of sincerity and truth.*⁶²

Colossians 2:20-23 "Do Not Touch, Do Not Taste, Do Not Handle"

²⁰ Therefore, if you died with Christ from the basic principles of the world, why, as though living in the world, do you subject yourselves to regulations— ²¹ "Do not touch, do not taste, do not handle," ²² which all concern things which perish with the using—according to the commandments and doctrines of men? ²³ These things indeed have an appearance of wisdom in self-imposed religion, false humility, and neglect of the body, but are of no value against the indulgence of the flesh.

Assertion:

Many assume that *"do not touch, do not taste, do not handle"* must refer to the ritualistic Old Testament Laws. Is that really what Paul is talking about?

Response:

It's just another example of man-made rulings and traditions getting in the way of the word of God, as is clearly stated in verse 22: *"according to the commandments and doctrines of men."* This section has nothing to do with the Law of God.

The regulations of verse 20 are likely one of two things: Rabbinic regulations limiting one's lifestyle further than the biblical Law distinguishes, or ascetic thought and practices—activities performed with the intention of making oneself miserable and thus able to focus better on God and spiritual things instead of earthly/material things.

---

⁶² 1 Corinthians 5:7-8

Things that ascetics would abstain from include food, drink, and pleasurable activities, including sexual relations, even with one's wife.

The Gnostics worshiped a goddess called Sophia (meaning "wisdom" in Greek). They claimed to have received true wisdom ("sophia") and knowledge ("gnosis") from her. The Gnostics took their name from the word "gnosis" itself. However, they also claimed to believe in parts of the Bible. The heresy of Gnosticism was infiltrating the Church at this time, and Paul possibly argued against them in this passage. The Gnostics certainly had the appearance of wisdom and religiosity, but they did not have the truth. They believed that by diminishing their carnal appetite, they would become less material and more spiritual. If this application is correct, Paul states that such practices *"are of no value against the indulgence of the flesh."* Put plainly, continuously beating down the body does not curb appetites for carnal pleasure. However, having *"died with Christ"* (verse 20) will help you control such appetites.

1 Timothy

1 Timothy 1:9-10 "The Law Was Not Made For a Righteous Person"

⁹ knowing this: that the law is not made for a righteous person, but for [the] lawless and insubordinate, for [the] ungodly and for sinners, for [the] unholy and profane, for murderers of fathers and murderers of mothers, for manslayers, ¹⁰ for fornicators, for sodomites, for kidnappers, for liars, for perjurers, and if there is any other thing that is contrary to sound doctrine...

Assertion:

The Law is made for evil people, but under Christ, we're cleansed from evil and are righteous in Christ. Therefore, we don't need the Law.

Response:

The Law exists as God's standard of right and wrong and shows us where we cross that line. Like any other law code in history, laws only exist to delineate what is acceptable and unacceptable. The Law serves no practical purpose to the person doing what is acceptable. The Law is only relevant to the person who wants to transgress. Therefore, the Law was made for those who are transgressors.

The Law of God is a standard by which we define right and wrong, righteousness and sin. It is a mirror by which we can evaluate ourselves. In this way, the Law was given to sinners to show them the way.

1 Timothy 4:1-3 "Forbidding to Abstain From Foods"

¹ Now the Spirit expressly says that in latter times some will depart from the faith, giving heed to deceiving spirits and doctrines of demons, ² speaking lies in hypocrisy, having their own conscience seared with a hot iron, ³ forbidding to marry, and commanding to abstain from foods which God created to be received with thanksgiving by those who believe and know the truth.

Assertion:

Abstaining from foods is usually assumed to be a reference to the dietary laws of the Old Testament, but is that what context tells us?

Response:

Much like the entry on **Colossians 2:20-23,** this also appears to be dealing with asceticism. Asceticism is the belief that abstaining from fleshly pleasures such as meats, alcohol, marriage, etc., will diminish the flesh and thus empower the spirit. Paul attributes their beliefs to *"doctrines of demons."* He says that their conscience is seared with a hot iron, which may be a way of saying that these individuals have been branded as belonging to the aforementioned demonic spirits.

Occasionally, people will pick out the words *"obtain from foods"* and try to correlate that with the biblical dietary Laws. Firstly, the context here simply does not support it because God has not forbidden marriage, which is also referenced in the same sentence. Also, Paul specifies food that God has created to be received. But if God says explicitly that meat ought not to be eaten, He has not created it to be received as food.

This passage is the necessary context for the following passage we address.

1 Timothy 4:4-5 "Nothing is to be Refused"

⁴ For every creature of God is good, and nothing is to be refused if it is received with thanksgiving; ⁵ for it is sanctified by the word of God and prayer.

Assertion:

Generally, this is read as follows: "Every creature of God is good and able to be received (understood as "eaten") if done so with thanksgiving." Is that what Paul is talking about?

Response:

Please see the previous section addressing **1 Timothy 4:1-3** before moving into this section.

This is a favorite amongst those trying to justify that every animal is clean. Please notice that the verse specifies that the good meat is *"of God"* and *"is sanctified by the word of God,"* not only by prayer. A prayer will not sanctify that which God has already called an abomination, in the same way that a prayer cannot sanctify idolatry, child sacrifice, homosexuality, etc. The word of God defines what is sanctified (made holy, set apart) and what is not in **Leviticus 11** and **Deuteronomy 14**. It is in **Leviticus 11**, the chapter all about the dietary Laws, where we find the famous phrase *"be holy, for I am holy."*[63]

---

[63] Leviticus 11:44-45

Titus

Titus 1:15 "To The Pure, All Things Are Pure"

15 To the pure all things are pure, but to those who are defiled and unbelieving nothing is pure; but even their mind and conscience are defiled.

Assertion:

We are all made "pure" in Christ, and thus, whatever we do is pure. Therefore, we cannot break the Law even if we try.

Because of the language of "pure" and "defiled," some people claim that Paul is specifically deleting regulations in the Law regarding clean and unclean.

Let's see if either of these perspectives fit.

Response:

Context is always helpful: **Titus 1:13b-16** *13 Therefore rebuke them (Cretans) [64]sharply, that they may be sound in the faith, 14 not giving heed to Jewish fables and commandments of men who turn from the truth. 15 To the pure all things are pure, but to those who are defiled and unbelieving nothing is pure; but even their mind and conscience are defiled. 16 They profess to know God, but in works they deny [Him], being abominable, disobedient, and disqualified for every good work."*

---

[64] *Titus 1:12*

Paul was writing to Titus to address a specific problem with the Cretans. He instructs that Titus should rebuke the Cretans so that they do not give heed to *"Jewish fables and commandments of men,"* that is, man-made traditions contrary to the biblical doctrine Paul is teaching. He says that they profess to know God, but by their works, they deny Him.

Simply put, these are a bunch of people who claim a title of religiosity, wrongly attributing God's name to it. They'd created a system of religious rules not found in scripture. Despite these problems, despite projecting a pious appearance, their works show them to be what they are, namely, defiled.

Paul continues by stating that to the pure, all things are pure. What he is not saying is that literally anything and everything is pure. Murder, adultery, idolatry, and the like are not pure. Rather, those who operate from the foundation of faith are pure in whatever they do. Similarly, those who operate from a foundation of religious hypocrisy are defiled in all that they do. This is comparable to what Paul tells the Romans, *"Whatever is not from faith is sin."*[65] Likewise, Jesus teaches us that what comes from the heart defiles a person (see **Matthew 15:18-20, Mark 7:20-23**) not outward expressions.

---

[65] Romans 14:23

Hebrews

The book of Hebrews is a complex book rooted heavily in the Old Testament. Thus, properly explaining it would take much longer than appropriate for a reference book like this. The following is a summary of how I understand and would explain this section of the book of Hebrews so that we have a background to the sections we address. This short paragraph does not do justice to the intricacies of the Book of Hebrews:

Jesus is the priest from heaven, serving the Tabernacle in heaven. The Levitical priesthood is the earthly replica of that, *"see that you make all things according to the pattern (of heaven) that I have shown you on the mountain."* [66] So if the priesthood is transferred, there must also be a transference of the law (see **Hebrews 7:12**). It is now Jesus, as the high priest in heaven, teaching us and leading us to the Law of God as the Levites did (see **Deuteronomy 33:10**). Our citizenship is in heaven (see **Philippians 3:20**) so our high priest must be also. The Levitical system remains unchanged. However, it was bound to physical life. Jesus, our spiritual high priest in heaven, can transform, purify, and intercede for people in ways much deeper and more significant than just the physical realm, reforming us from the inside out.

Hebrews 7:11-12 "Change of the Law"

[11] *Therefore, if perfection were through the Levitical priesthood for under it the*

---

[66] **Hebrews 8:5, Exodus 25:40**

people received the Law, what further need was there that another priest should rise according to the order of Melchizedek and not be called according to the order of Aaron? [12] For the priesthood being changed, of necessity there is also a change of the law.

Assertion:

If the Law cannot attain perfection and has been changed, why would we still observe the Old Testament Law? Let's find out.

Response:

Most Bibles read "perfection" instead of "completeness" and "changed" instead of "transferred" in these two verses, probably due to translator bias. These Greek words would be more accurately translated as "completeness" and "transferred," respectively. Thus, we could read: *Therefore, if completeness were through the Levitical priesthood (for under it the people received the Law), what further need was there that another priest should rise according to the order of Melchizedek, and not be called according to the order of Aaron? For the priesthood being transferred, of necessity there is also a transference of the law.*

With this adjustment, we can now see that the Levitical priesthood could not create a complete change in the individuals it served. Another priest must arise from another order, and the task of interceding before God on behalf of the people must be transferred to this priest, who can complete the task given to him. This new priest and new order is Jesus, in the order of Melchizedek.

The *"law"* mentioned above and the *"commandment"* [67] are clarified by **Hebrews 7:15-16** which defines these words specifically as the "fleshly commandment" (the genealogical requirements of the priesthood). The law/commandment has nothing to do with whether the priesthood should exist. Instead, it refers to the genealogical requirement for priestly service. The Levitical system was limited to the flesh from the start, as it comprised members of Aaron's genealogy and served in the earthly domain. Therefore, there has been a transference (not a transformation) of the law regarding priesthood to

---

[67] **Hebrews 7:16**

the order of Melchizedek, *"of whom we have much to say and hard to explain."*[68]

Hebrews 7:18-19 "Annulling of the Former Commandment"

18 For on the one hand there is an annulling of the former commandment because of its weakness and unprofitableness, 19 for the law made nothing perfect; on the other hand, there is the bringing in of a better hope, through which we draw near to God.

Assertion:

Many readers in this section lack context and assume that the *"former commandment"* that is annulled is the Old Testament Law. Let's explore:

Response:

The context here is the priesthood; therefore, the "commandment" mentioned also refers to the priesthood. The text says that the former commandment regarding priesthood was annulled (rejected), but how? Jesus was rejected from being a Levitical priest because he was not a Levite. He was rejected from the Levitical order, the *"former commandment."* Therefore, if he has become a priest, then by necessity, he has become a priest of a different order. He was made a priest with an oath (see **Hebrews 7:20-21**) after the order of Melchizedek, and not according to the order of Aaron, for Aaron's descendants are all mortal (see **Hebrews 7:23-34**).

The priesthood of the genealogical requirement was profitable for cleansing the outer (physical) man but was unprofitable for cleansing the inner man because it was not designed to do such a thing—yet we still needed to have our inner man cleansed. The genealogical requirement could not make a person complete; on the other hand, there is the bringing in of a better hope (Jesus), through which we draw near to God.

---

[68] Hebrews 5:11

Hebrews 7:28 "The Word of the Oath, Which Came After the Law"

28 For the law appoints as high priests men who have weakness, but the word of the oath, which came after the law, appoints the Son who has been perfected forever.

Assertion:

Unlike the Levites, the Son, who came after the Law, has been perfected. Therefore, we don't need the Old Testament anymore.

Response:

This does not mean that the law is useless or nullified. It says that the law appointed men to be priests, but men are mortal and flawed. The Levitical priests, being merely human, needed to make atonement for themselves before they could atone for the people (see **Leviticus 16:11**, about the Day of Atonement). (see **Hebrews 9:12 and 10:4**) Because Jesus is immortal and sinless, his priesthood is greater than the Levitical system, in that he has no sins of his own to atone for. The "word of the oath" appoints the son of God, who does not have these shortcomings. In this way, the latter is superior. Simply put, the problem lies with man's weakness, not with the Law of God.

Hebrews 8:6-7 "Better Covenant"

6 But now He has obtained a more excellent ministry, inasmuch as He is also Mediator of a better covenant, which was established on better promises. 7 For if that first covenant had been faultless, then no place would have been sought for a second.

Assertion:

It has been said that the first covenant was faulty, and the Son has established a better covenant. Therefore, we don't need the old covenant anymore.

Response:

Jesus' "priestliness" is superior to the earthly priesthood because it *can* purify a human heart – something the Levitical system can't do, nor was it ever designed to do. The covenant of Moses is inferior to the covenant of Jesus since Moses' Law would not change our hearts. In contrast, the covenant brought by Jesus, administered through the Holy Spirit (in the new covenant), can change our hearts. Although the Law remained written on stones and scrolls, it was also written on human hearts so that we would have a desire to obey and not merely an obedience done out of fear of punishment (see **2 Corinthians 3:3, Jeremiah 31:33, Ezekiel 36:26-27**).

It is important to note that, again, the covenant mentioned above in context is not the entirety of the Mosaic Law but the priesthood that officiated it. Notice also that it says He found fault with the priests. The covenant of priesthood was based on the priesthood from heaven; it is perfect in every way. The problem is not the covenant itself; the problem is that the priests were mortal humans and fraught with sin. This contrasts with Jesus, our heavenly high priest who never sinned and can officiate perfectly.

The first covenant could indeed cleanse the flesh (see **Hebrews 9:13-15a**). However, since the people still had sin and needed spiritual cleansing, another covenant was needed to cleanse their hearts. This is the purpose of the new and better covenant. Thus, Jesus acts as our sinless heavenly high priest who can cleanse us.

Hebrews 8:13 "Made the First Obsolete"

¹³In that He says, "A new covenant," He has made the first obsolete. Now what is becoming obsolete and growing old is ready to vanish away.

Assertion:

If the first covenant is growing old and vanishing, why should we pay any heed to the Old Testament?

Response:

Firstly, there are some translation issues to address in this verse. Obsolete, which occurs twice, comes from the Greek word παλαιόω, palaioō simply meaning "to become old." So also does the word already translated "old," which comes from γηράσκω, gēraskō. Both of these are verbs describing the aging process somewhat synonymously. Additionally, the word "covenant" does not appear in Greek, though it is likely a good assumption based on verse 10.

The verse would probably translate more directly: *"In that He says, "A new," He has made the first old. Now what is aging and growing old is ready to vanish away."*

These translation notes may or may not make any functional difference in interpretation, but I feel they are valuable to note.

As with the rest of the surrounding text, I believe the covenant in question is that of the priesthood specifically, not the entirety of the Mosaic Covenant.

When the new covenant of priesthood is ratified, the old does not automatically get removed but becomes unnecessary and insignificant. The earthly Levitical priesthood reflects that which exists in heaven, which Moses copied (see **Exodus 25:40, Hebrews 8:5**). It served the purpose of cleansing the physical bodies to enter into the physical presence of God. The new priesthood with Jesus officiating in heaven can cleanse the heart of a person to enter into the spiritual presence of God.

This reality does not remove the Levitical system, but it does render it rather pointless. Who would not choose the greater priesthood?

Hebrews 9:9-10 "Fleshly Ordinances Imposed Until the Reformation"

⁹ It (Day of Atonement Ceremony) was symbolic for the present time in which both gifts and sacrifices are offered which cannot make him who performed the service perfect in regard to the conscience— ¹⁰ concerned only with foods and drinks, various washings, and fleshly ordinances imposed until the time of reformation.

It has been said that this verse abolished the "old Law" because it is carnal, and it becomes replaced at "the time of reformation." Maybe we don't understand the subject matter of this section.

Response:

The Levitical priesthood was symbolic of the priesthood in heaven. Everything that was done in it was a physical representation of that which is in heaven, a copy and shadow performed by mortal man. It was only profitable to the flesh (the body)Its bodily nature could not bring a spiritual cleansing. It did its job well, but its job was limited to physical life. This does not inherently make the Levitical system bad; it is simply limited.

"This was symbolic for the present time." This proves that the Temple and the services represent Jesus' work. The earthly Temple is not merely an impotent shadowy hologram. Rather, the earthly Temple system vividly represents realities about Christ and his work.

Regarding verse 10, these are all things that pertain to the body and affect physical behavior but cannot affect the heart. Like much of the Law, these are rules to modify behavior, but they exist and function independently of the person's heart. This is the emphasis in the coming of the new covenant: when works unite with the heart. This is complete faith, spelled out in the new covenant.

Hebrews 9:16-17 "Death of the Testator"

16 For where there is a testament, there must also of necessity be the death of the testator. 17 For a testament is in force after men are dead, since it has no power at all while the testator lives.

Assertion:

It has been said that the Old Testament died with the Jesus's death.

Response:

This all stems from poor translation. Young's Literal Translation (YLT) does a better job of explaining this verse:

"For where a covenant [is], the death of the covenant-victim to come in is necessary, for a covenant over dead victims [is] steadfast, since it is no force at all when the covenant-victim liveth," [69]

Covenants were often made with a sacrifice, a "covenant-victim" (see **Genesis 15:9-11, Exodus 24:5-8, Psalm 50:5, Jeremiah 34:18-19, Zechariah 9:11**). Until the sacrifice was made, the covenant was not in force. Thus, when Jesus died as the sacrifice, his covenant was put into effect. Recall when Jesus said, *"This is my blood of the new covenant..."*[70] The evening before his death. Now, with this understanding, consider the context of the rest of this section in Hebrews:

"[16] For where there is a covenant, there must also of necessity be the death of the covenant victim. [17] For a covenant is in force after dead victims since it has no power at all while the covenant victim lives. [18] Therefore not even the first covenant was dedicated without blood. [19] For when Moses had spoken every precept to all the people according to the law, he took the blood of calves and goats, with water, scarlet wool, and hyssop, and sprinkled both the book itself and all the people, [20] saying, "This is the blood of the covenant which God has commanded you." [21] Then likewise he sprinkled with blood both the tabernacle and all the vessels of the ministry." [71] (see also: **Exodus 24:3-8**)

This section does not describe the "death" of the Old Covenant. It says that the Old Covenant, the New Covenant, and basically any other biblical covenant is ratified by the blood of a "covenant victim." With Moses, it was calves and goats, but the blood of Jesus Christ ratified the New Covenant. The point for us to gain from this contrast is to see how much greater the sacrifice of Christ is than what came before! As it says a few verses later: *Therefore [it was] necessary that the copies of the things in the heavens should be purified with these, but the heavenly things themselves with beter sacrifices than these.*

---

[69] Hebrews 9:16-17 YLT98

[70] Matthew 26:28

[71] Hebrews 9:16-21

Hebrews 10:1-4 "Impossible for the Blood of Bulls and Goats"

¹ For the law, having a shadow of the good things to come, and not the very image of the things, can never with these same sacrifices, which they offer continually year by year, make those who approach perfect. ² For then would they not have ceased to be offered? For the worshipers, once purified, would have had no more consciousness of sins. ³ But in those sacrifices there is a reminder of sins every year. ⁴ For it is not possible that the blood of bulls and goats could take away sins.

Assertion:

Because *"it is not possible that the blood of bulls and goats could take away sins,"* then the Old Testament system was faulty, useless, and must be discarded.

Response:

Regarding verse 2, the author is now speaking exclusively of sin sacrifices—no other sacrifices, gifts, or offerings. Only sin sacrifices. Though these sin sacrifices were made, they still could not cleanse the person's conscience. They could only cleanse the flesh to allow the individual to enter the physical presence of God.

The earthly priesthood and sacrificial system is not useless; it serves in the physical realm and thus also is a reflection of the heavenly realm. However, because it is only a dim copy, it represents something greater than it is, meaning it cannot carry out the fullest purpose that it demonstrates. However, showing the image is a constant reminder of sin every year as it is acted out. This does not make the physical priestly system void, but it does make it pale compared to the reality of the heavenly priesthood it represents.

---

[72] Hebrews 9:23

Hebrews 10:8-9 "Take Away the First, Establish the Second"

⁸ Previously saying, "Sacrifice and offering, burnt offerings, and [offerings] for sin You did not desire, nor had pleasure [in them]" which are offered according to the law, ⁹ then He said, "Behold, I have come to do Your will, O God." He takes away the first that He may establish the second.

Assertion:

God, through Jesus, took away the old system to make room for the new.

Response:

Jesus' priestly ministry is infinitely more capable than the Levitical priestly ministry that came before it. Jesus' Priesthood can change the hearts of mankind, while Levites can only change the physical being by means of the blood of sacrifice animals. God never desired to stop the sanctification of mankind at the skin level. God wanted reformation much deeper. Therefore, God is not ultimately pleased by *"Sacrifice and offering, burnt offerings, and [offerings] for sin."*

This line in verse 9 is drawn from **Psalm 40:7-8**, which says, *"Then I said, 'Behold, I come; In the scroll of the book it is written of me. I delight to do Your will, O my God, And Your Law is within my heart.'"* We know that *"Your Law is within my heart"* is a sign of the new covenant according to **Ezekiel 36:26-27** and **Jeremiah 33:31-34**. Thus, the *"delight to do [His] will"* is to manifest His Law in all our hearts. To move the words of the covenant from the tablets of stone to the tablet of the heart.

This is what is so significant about the Priesthood of Jesus. Jesus's sacrifice and the Spirit of God working in our hearts can change our inner person to delight in doing His will and having His Law in our hearts in a way that stones and scrolls never could. In *this* way, He takes away the first to establish the second.

Hebrews 10:20 "New and Living Way"

²⁰ by a new and living way which He consecrated for us, through the veil, that is, His flesh,

Assertion:

The *"new and living way"* replaces the old way.

Response:

People often read the phrase *"new and living way"* and assume it refers to the new covenant. While this assumption is correct, it implies that it makes the old covenant outdated, useless, and dead.

The fact that this verse is not even a complete sentence should clue us in to look at the context. *Therefore, brethren, having boldness to enter the Holiest by the blood of Jesus, by a new and living way which He consecrated for us, through the veil, that is, His flesh, and having a High Priest over the house of God, let us draw near with a true heart in full assurance of faith, having our hearts sprinkled from an evil conscience and our bodies washed with pure water.* [73]

In other words, brethren, we have the boldness to enter the Holiest by the blood of Jesus, by a new heart and a new spirit and repentance from dead works—the living way which he consecrated for us as our heavenly high priest. This is why God lets us draw near with a "true heart" in "faith" because our hearts are cleansed from evil thoughts and intentions.

The point of the section is that by the blood of Jesus, we have attained the ultimate perfection that the Levitical system could only imitate.

---

[73] Hebrews 10:19-22

James

James 2:10 "Stumble in One Point, Guilty of All"

¹⁰ For whoever shall keep the whole Law, and yet stumble in one point, he is guilty of all.

Assertion:

It's been said that if you sin at any point in the Law, you're guilty of all sins - thus concluding that there's no reason to even try.

Response:

Let's put this passage back in context.

⁸ If you really fulfill the royal Law according to the Scripture, "You shall love your neighbor as yourself," you do well; ⁹ but if you show partiality, you commit sin and are convicted by the Law as transgressors. ¹⁰ For whoever shall keep the whole Law, and yet stumble in one point, he is guilty of all. ¹¹ For He who said, "Do not commit adultery," also said, "Do not murder." Now if you do not commit adultery, but you do murder, you have become a transgressor of the Law. ¹² So speak and so do as those who will be judged by the Law of liberty. ¹³ For judgment is without mercy to the one who has shown no mercy. Mercy triumphs over judgment.

James teaches that stumbling at even one point of the Law makes you guilty; in the same way, breaking one chain link renders the chain ineffective. Once a person knowingly transgresses a single point, all he has done right, his righteousness, becomes irrelevant, and he depends on the mercy of the Judge (see also **Ezekiel 18:24-28**). Therefore, because of this, he teaches that we should act like those about to be judged. He says, *"Judgment is without mercy to the one who has shown no mercy."* This is comparable to when Jesus says, *"For with what judgment you judge, you will be judged; and with the measure you use, it will be measured back to you"* [75] and even clearer in his parable about the unforgiving servant.

[23] *Therefore the kingdom of heaven is like a certain king who wanted to settle accounts with his servants.* [24] *And when he had begun to settle accounts, one was brought to him who owed him ten thousand talents.* [25] *But as he was not able to pay, his master commanded that he be sold, with his wife and children and all that he had, and that payment be made.* [26]*The servant therefore fell down before him, saying, 'Master, have patience with me, and I will pay you all.'* [27] *Then the master of that servant was moved with compassion, released him, and forgave him the debt.* [28] *"But that servant went out and found one of his fellow servants who owed him a hundred denarii; and he laid hands on him and took him by the throat, saying, 'Pay me what you owe!'* [29] *So his fellow servant fell down at his feet and begged him, saying, 'Have patience with me, and I will pay you all.'* [30] *And he would not, but went and threw him into prison till he should pay the debt.* [31] *So when his fellow servants saw what had been done, they were very grieved, and came and told their master all that had been done.* [32] *Then his master, after he had called him, said to him, 'You wicked servant! I forgave you all that debt because you begged me.* [33] *Should you not also have had compassion on your fellow servant, just as I had pity on you?'* [34] *And his master was angry, and delivered him to the torturers until he should pay all that was due to him.* [35] *"So My heavenly Father also will do to you if each of you, from his heart, does not forgive his brother his trespasses."*

In summation, James teaches in this section the same thing taught by Jesus and by biblical authors before him: that we must learn to be merciful and not seek to judge others because the amount of mercy we give to others is the same amount of mercy we will receive. We all need a lot of mercy!

---

[74] James 2:8-13

[75] Matthew 7:2, Matthew 18:23-35

About the Author

Shaun Howe is a regular guy who works as an electrician, coming home to his wife and five children every evening. He enjoys many hobbies including studying scripture. Shaun has been passionate about scripture for around two decades, and hopes that some of the fruit of that labor of love may be borne out through this book.

www.ingramcontent.com/pod-product-compliance
Lightning Source LLC
Chambersburg PA
CBHW051538120626
46551CB00013B/1270